Chinese Investment in the United States: Recent Trends in Real Estate, Industry, and Investment Promotion

Table of Contents

List of Tables and Figures

Executive Summary

Between 2011 and 2013, the value of China's mergers and acquisitions (M&A) in the United States exceeded the value of U.S. M&A deals in China.[1] While it is too early to call this a permanent turning point, Chinese companies are poised to deepen their presence in the United States. Despite a recent economic slowdown, China remains a dominant goods exporter and is growing at a faster clip than the rest of the world. China's central bank holds some $4 trillion in foreign exchange reserves, and Chinese companies and wealthy individuals are eager to diversify their assets overseas.

Although there is a steady stream of analysis on Chinese outbound investment, less well documented is how this investment is distributed among different industries and localities across the United States.[*] Highly publicized deals, such as Shuanghui Group's $4.72 billion acquisition of Smithfield Group in 2013 and Lenovo's $2.95 billion acquisition of Motorola Mobility in 2014, can obscure the bigger picture. Smaller transactions are less consequential for the national economy, yet may exert a tangible impact on states and local communities. Investment patterns are determined to a large degree by China's economic policies and corporate strategies. Viewing Chinese investment from this broader perspective helps shed light on other important issues, such as Chinese purchases of U.S. homes, the granting of EB-5 visas,[†] and bilateral research exchanges.

To explore these issues, Commission staff conducted a series of telephone and e-mail interviews with over a dozen U.S. state officials between August 2014 and February 2015.[‡] These interviews were supplemented by analysis of state government websites, media and industry reports, as well as quantitative data on trade and investment flows. The paper's principal conclusions are:

- The investment promotion efforts of U.S. states vary widely. Commission staff counted 25 states with representative offices in China. Among these, states from the U.S. South, such as Georgia and the Carolinas, conduct very active outreach. Michigan and California temporarily closed and recently reopened their China offices, substituting wholly government-run entities with public-private partnerships. Back in the United States, Maryland has developed a research incubator at College Park primarily to host Chinese firms. In contrast, energy-abundant states in the U.S. Southwest receive substantial Chinese investment but do not appear to run major outreach programs. New Jersey uses trade fairs to pitch its industries to Chinese investors.

- China's new leadership has reduced restrictions on outbound investment over the past year, while a gradual recovery is raising the appeal of the U.S. economy in the eyes of foreign investors. That suggests Chinese investment in the United States will continue to expand, particularly as Chinese companies and individuals accrue wealth and China's central bank attempts to diversify the country's large foreign exchange reserves.

- Wealthy individuals and corporate entities from China are investing extensively in U.S. residential and commercial property, foremost in wealthy coastal cities such as New York and Los Angeles. China's commercial investors range from Dalian Wanda Group Co. Ltd., China's largest commercial property company and the world's largest cinema chain operator, to state-owned insurance companies. Private individuals, many of them tied to China's economic elite, prefer to buy U.S. properties using all cash and treat them as secondary residences to generate rental income. The influx of Chinese investment is buoying local property markets, but it also presents a challenge to state officials who struggle to administer the volume of deals and prevent misconduct.

- A related concern is China's extensive use of the EB-5 visa program, which allows foreign nationals and their family members to receive conditional green cards in exchange for an investment of $1 million, or $500,000 in geographic areas of the United States that have high unemployment rates—also known as

---

* For additional analysis of Chinese investment in the United States, see Iacob Koch-Weser and Owen Haacke, *China Investment Corporation: Recent Developments in Performance, Strategy, and Governance* (U.S.-China Economic and Security Review Commission, June 2013); U.S.-China Economic and Security Review Commission, *2013 Annual Report to Congress*, November 2013, Chapter 1.2. These reports can be accessed at *http://www.uscc.gov*.

† The EB-5 visa provides a method of obtaining a green card for foreign nationals who invest money in the United States.

‡ Interviewees were from the states of Arkansas, California, Colorado, Georgia, Iowa, Maryland, Michigan, Mississippi, Missouri, New Jersey, North Carolina, Oregon, Pennsylvania, and South Carolina. Not all states were available to be interviewed for this paper.

Investor Targeted Employment Areas (TEAs). The applicants' investments are certified by authorities at the local level, and the resulting certificates are used to apply for a conditional green card at the federal level with U.S. Citizenship and Immigration Services (USCIS). The program has been flooded by Chinese applicants, to the extent that the applicant vacancies were filled prematurely in fiscal year 2014. Instances of fraud and lax regulation have cast doubt on the ability of local authorities to screen Chinese EB-5 investors properly.

- Although EB-5 investors can act on their own, they often turn to Immigrant Investor Regional Centers ("Regional Centers") to help identify and vet projects that qualify for the EB-5 program, and to seek assistance with domestic and international compliance work. Regional Centers are not subject to regulation by U.S. state governments. USCIS approves the Regional Centers but explicitly states it does not endorse their behavior or guarantee their compliance with U.S. securities laws. In addition, TEAs are fairly easy to qualify for, even in California, a state that has standardized its TEA regulations using Census tracts.

- China's business activities in the United States encompass a broad spectrum of industries, from light manufacturing operations that capitalize on cheap U.S. energy and farm goods, to corporate acquisitions in the automotive sector and research and development (R&D)-driven projects in healthcare and pharmaceuticals. Chinese investments exert divergent effects on job creation and involve a mix of private and state-owned companies. State officials have noted Chinese investors are often not as experienced as other international investors, and prefer to receive support from local officials over hiring private consultants.

Several aspects of Chinese investment merit closer consideration by U.S. policymakers:

- Regulation of the EB-5 visa program could be improved in view of the rapid influx of Chinese investors and repeated instances of poorly executed and fraudulent EB-5 projects.

- Federal programs could better assist local governments in identifying opportunities for China-focused investment promotion, as well as in assessing risks to critical infrastructure and technologies.

- If implemented within an appropriate regulatory framework, local research incubators can contribute to U.S.-China R&D cooperation and deliver economic and societal benefits to both countries.

- As Chinese investment in labor- and energy-intensive U.S. industries increases, adherence to U.S. labor and environmental laws—across all U.S. states—will be a priority issue.

- Foreign investment from China into the United States is not sufficient to "rebalance" the bilateral economic relationship in terms of bilateral market access, goods trade, and the overall balance of payments.

This paper begins with a review of trends in Chinese outbound investment policy and the general composition of Chinese investment in the United States. Subsequent sections consider Chinese investments in real estate and a sample of U.S. industries. The final sections examine state outreach efforts more closely, and conclude with implications for the United States.

Trends in China's Outbound Investment

China's Monetary Policy Dilemma and Outbound Investment Regime

Government statistics on foreign direct investment (FDI) can be unreliable, not least in China's case.[*] There is enough evidence, though, to identify key trends. China continues to accumulate vast foreign exchange reserves. As of October 2014, the People's Bank of China (PBOC) held $3.89 trillion. This was a slight drop from the $3.99 trillion reported in June, suggesting there were net outflows in the third quarter of 2014.[2] But prior to that, from the third quarter of 2013 to the second quarter of 2014, China's foreign exchange reserves grew by nearly half a trillion dollars in value.[3] Already at year-end 2013, China's total reserves (including gold) were greater than the next six largest reserve-holders (including the United States) combined.[4]

These outsized reserves are a byproduct of strict currency and capital controls imposed by China's central bank to insulate the domestic financial sector and slow appreciation of the renminbi (RMB) against the dollar. The challenge for the Chinese government is to enhance the value of these reserves, the majority of which are invested in dollar-denominated financial instruments such as U.S. treasuries and government agency bonds. Treasuries and other bonds offer low yields and expose China to the depreciation of the dollar against the RMB.

China has had some success diversifying its foreign assets. According to China's State Administration of Foreign Exchange (SAFE), between the first quarter of 2011 and the second quarter of 2014, China's cumulative assets from outbound direct investment increased nearly twofold, from $323.4 billion to $640.2 billion (see Figure 1). China has accrued additional foreign assets through outbound trade credit, lending, and currency and deposits ($1.25 trillion as of June 2014).[5] A portion of the currency and deposits goes to Hong Kong, where it is used to make Hong Kong-origin outbound investments.[6] China is also becoming a net outbound investor. In an October 2014 report, the Center for China & Globalization[†] projected Chinese outbound investment flows to reach $120 billion in 2014, exceeding projected inbound flows.[7]

And yet, this diversification process is proceeding at a slow pace. As of June 2014, 63.3 percent of China's total foreign assets consisted of foreign exchange reserves, compared to 70.1 percent three years earlier.[8]

Alongside piecemeal reforms to reduce the rate of accumulation of foreign exchange, China is likely to respond to its monetary policy dilemma by reinvesting foreign currency abroad. Under President Xi Jinping, China recently undertook the most significant reforms to its outbound investment policies in over a decade:

- At the conclusion of the Third Plenary Session of the 18th Party Congress in November 2013, the government issued a document ("Third Plenum Decision") that proposes to reduce administrative approvals for various types of economic activity.[‡]

- In December 2013, China's State Council ordered its officials to "significantly liberalize outbound FDI policies" via an update to the Government Approval of Investment Projects Catalogue (GAIPC).[9] The new GAIPC redefines the roles of the primary regulatory agencies: the National Development and Reform Commission (NDRC) and the Ministry of Commerce (MOFCOM).[10] In October 2014, the

---

[*] China's Ministry of Commerce (MOFCOM) publishes FDI figures that differ from the investment flows recorded by the State Administration of Foreign Exchange (SAFE), a subsidiary of the central bank that publishes China's international investment position (IIP) on a quarterly basis. MOFCOM's FDI statistics have been problematic because they are based largely on administrative project approvals and often only track the first (predominately Hong Kong), and not final, destination for outflows. U.S. government statistics on inbound investment from Chinese companies are difficult to accept at face value as well, because the U.S. government neglects Chinese FDI coming through Hong Kong and locations other than the Mainland. Moreover, this FDI is rendered volatile by intracompany flows and the capital allocation decisions of corporate treasurers based on exchange rate expectations, tax holidays, and other factors. For further discussion, see Daniel Rosen and Thilo Hanemann, *New Realities in the U.S.-China Investment Relationship* (Rhodium Group, April 29, 2014). *http://rhg.com/notes/newrealities-in-the-us-china-investment-relationship.*

[†] The Center for China & Globalization (CCG) identifies itself as an independent think tank based in China. Its partners include the Harvard University Ash Center for Democratic Governance and Innovation and the National University of Singapore. The CCG's research focuses on the effects of globalization on the Chinese economy. The organization has offices in Beijing, Guangzhou, Qingdao, Shenzhen, Hong Kong, and New York. Center for China & Globalization, "About." *http://en.ccg.org.cn/.*

[‡] For more information, see Nargiza Salidjanova and Iacob Koch-Weser, *The Third Plenum Economic Reform Proposals: A Scorecard* (U.S.-China Economic and Security Review Commission, November 19, 2013). This report can be accessed at *http://www.uscc.gov.*

State Council declared it would eliminate outbound direct investment approvals altogether in the next iteration of the GAIPC.[11]

- Based on the State Council directive, NDRC and MOFCOM have formalized their reforms to outbound investment regulation. Under new rules issued in April 2014 ("Order 9"), approval by the NDRC is only required when an investment exceeds $1 billion or the project involves a sensitive country, region, or sector.* Outbound investments exceeding $300 million or made by a centrally administered state-owned enterprise (SOE) need only be filed with the central-level NDRC. Investments less than $300 million need only be filed with the provincial-level NDRC.[12]

- Under a measure issued in September 2014 ("Order 3"), approval by MOFCOM is now required strictly for outbound investments in sensitive countries, regions, or sectors, regardless of deal size. All other investments need only be filed: in the case of central SOEs, with MOFCOM at the central level; for all other domestic firms, with MOFCOM at the provincial level.[13]

**Figure 1: China's Foreign Assets (excluding Foreign Exchange Reserves)
(US$ billions)**

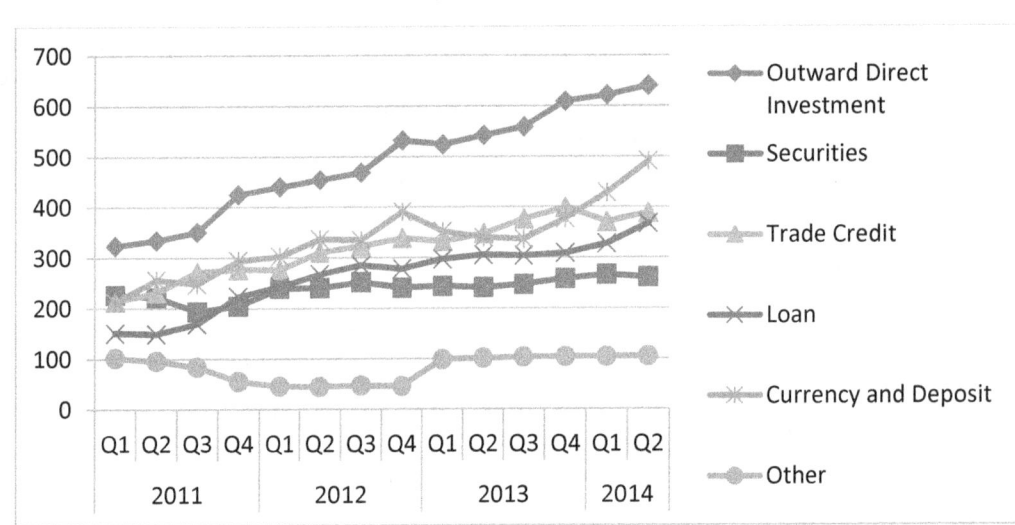

Source: China State Administration of Foreign Exchange, via CEIC.

These latest reforms are unlikely to open the floodgates to Chinese outbound investment. NDRC and MOFCOM officials could, for example, delay processing of applications submitted under the new filing system. Investors still require approval from SAFE, the authority responsible for the oversight of foreign exchange sourcing, conversion, and remittance. If need be, SAFE can use its authority to stem excessive outflows.[14]

Nonetheless, experts at Rhodium Group, an investment advisory firm, argue the new rules will "allow Chinese firms to close deals quicker and without government interference, which will help sustain recent outbound foreign direct investment growth, especially from the private sector."[15] The recent reforms build on China's "Go Out" policy

---

* According to O'Melveny and Myers LLP: " 'Sensitive sectors' are defined under Order 3 as those industries pertaining to export-restricted products and technologies or industries involving interests of more than a single nation or region. It is worth noting that these definitions in Order 3 are different than those in NDRC's Order 9. In addition to the countries and regions covered in Order 3, 'sensitive countries and regions' definitions under Order 9 also cover countries and regions embroiled in ongoing wars or riots. As for 'sensitive sectors,' Order 9 doesn't give a definition but only listed basic telecommunications, cross-border utilization of water, large-scale land development, main electricity transit line, electricity grid, news and media as examples of sensitive sectors." Wendy Pan, Ning Zhang, and Aaron Xin, *New MOFCOM Rules to Further Facilitate China Outbound Investments*, O'Melveny & Myers LLP, September 22, 2014. *http://www.omm.com/new-mofcom-rules-to-further-facilitate-china-outbound-investments/*.

directive, first promoted under the 10th Five-Year Plan (2001–2005). The directive gained further momentum in the wake of the 2007-2008 Global Financial Crisis.[*]

Chinese Investment in the Context of U.S. Capital Flows

The United States remains an attractive destination for foreign capital. According to statistics from the U.S. Bureau of Economic Analysis, the country's foreign liabilities—the money owed to foreign investors—increased by 11 percent in the second quarter of 2014, the highest quarterly, year-on-year increase since 2007.[16] In the heyday of the U.S. financial boom, financial derivatives bolstered U.S. capital inflows. Now, traditional forms of investment predominate. Portfolio investments—in funds, treasury bonds, and other debt securities—account for over half of U.S. foreign liabilities. Direct investment, comprising about one-fifth of U.S. foreign liabilities, is also growing at a fast rate. Within the direct investment category, the ratio of equity investments is rising,[17] suggesting a long-term commitment by foreign investors to the U.S. economy.

China's share of total U.S. FDI stock is marginal compared to the stock held by major economies like Japan and Germany. U.S. FDI stock in China, accumulating over decades, is also multiples larger than the sum of Chinese FDI in the United States.[18] Nonetheless, Rhodium Group estimates that in 2011 and 2012, Chinese FDI flows into the United States exceeded U.S. FDI flows into China. The trend is similar for bilateral M&A deals in 2011–2013.[19] Of the roughly $40 billion China has invested in the United States since the start of the century, more than half has entered in the last two years.[†]

The change in the balance of U.S.-China investment flows reflects market forces. China's labor force is shrinking and its companies and households are accumulating wealth. At the same time, the U.S. economy is recovering from the global recession. At 2.4 percent in 2014, U.S. real gross domestic product (GDP) growth is outperforming other advanced economies, such as Japan and the eurozone. Expert forecasts expect U.S. real GDP to grow by 3.6 percent (IMF) or 3.7 percent (Deutsche Bank) this year, bettering 2014 by about 1 percentage point.[20] The Federal Reserve's termination of its asset buying program ("quantitative easing") in October 2014, preceded by a gradual scaling back of the program,[21] has also had knock-on effects, such as the appreciation of the U.S. dollar against emerging market currencies.[22]

The fact remains, however, that China has not fully "rebalanced" its external accounts with the United States. The U.S. trade deficit in goods with China posted another record in 2014, impacted by Chinese policies to maximize exports and minimize imports through market intervention. China also maintains rigid capital controls and an unhealthy creditor relationship with the U.S. Treasury, effectively converting its excess savings into U.S. liabilities. In parallel, U.S. companies are finding it difficult to access China's emerging consumer class and services sector.[‡]

The Composition of Chinese Investment in the United States

A sanguine view of foreign investment is that it builds factories and creates jobs, but this view does not fully account for the nature of Chinese investment in the United States. A substantial amount is flowing into property; according to Rhodium Group, China's investment in U.S. real estate totaled $3.1 billion in 2014, up from $2.2 billion the year before.[23] Were it not for Lenovo's single purchase of Motorola, real estate would now be the leading sector for

---

[*] The "Go Out" directive encourages (select) Chinese enterprises to invest abroad in order to enhance China's resource security, acquire technology, seek new markets for Chinese goods and services, and improve corporate competitiveness. Implicitly linked to this directive are preferential access to credit, expedited approvals, and other incentives. For more information, see Nargiza Salidjanova, *Going Out: An Overview of China's Outward Foreign Direct Investment* (U.S.-China Economic and Security Review Commission, March 30, 2011). This report can be accessed at *http://www.uscc.gov*.

[†] According to data compiled by Rhodium Group, Chinese FDI in the United States hit a historic peak in the third quarter of 2013, at over $7 billion. The principal contributor was Shuanghui Group's $4.7 billion acquisition of Virginia-based Smithfield Group, the world's largest pork producer. (Shuanghui spent an additional $2.5 billion to assume Smithfield's debt.) The ensuing quarters saw an increase in transactions, though combined investment remained under $6 billion, as deals were smaller in size. Chinese investment rebounded in the third quarter of 2014, to $3.1 billion. Rhodium Group, *Chinese FDI in the United States: Q4 2014 and Full Year Update* (January 2015). *http://rhg.com/notes/chinese-fdi-in-the-united-states-q4-and-full-year-2014-update*; Rhodium Group, *Chinese FDI in the United States: Q3 2014 Update* (October 2014). *http://rhg.com/notes/chinese-fdi-in-the-united-states-q3-2014-update*.

[‡] For more information, see U.S.-China Economic and Security Review Commission, *2014 Annual Report to Congress*, November 2014, Chapter 1.1. This report can be accessed at *http://www.uscc.gov*.

Chinese direct investment into the United States. The real estate bonanza constitutes a global trend—Chinese outbound investment in this sector increased 200-fold between 2008 and June 2014. Outside the United States, China has concentrated its property purchases in London, Hong Kong, and Singapore.*

Further, Chinese investors in the United States prefer to buy existing assets through M&A, rather than create new assets through greenfield investment.† M&A deals have historically accounted for the bulk of Chinese investment deal value. Last year, they also comprised the majority of Chinese transactions.[24]

The companies Rhodium Group classifies as "private sector"‡ accounted for 76 percent of Chinese FDI transactions in the United States and 81 percent of total deal value in 2014, as investments by Chinese state-owned firms and sovereign players dropped sharply.[25] This is surprising, since virtually all Chinese companies in the Global Fortune 500 are state owned. The pendulum could reverse, however. China's state-owned energy companies, for example, could engage in a new round of purchases.[26] State-owned insurance companies have also received the green light by the Chinese government to increase their real estate investment overseas.[27] No less, several private companies, such as the turbine maker Goldwind Science & Technology Co., Ltd. and the pork producer Shuanghui Group, receive outbound investment support from China's state-owned banks in the form of long-term, low-interest loans.[28] Chinese state involvement may be present in a substantial percentage of cross-border deals and, therefore, is worth monitoring for its potential impact.

Real Estate Investment

Commercial Property Investment

Typically, China's real estate investments focus on residential properties, but commercial property deals are on the increase. Contrary to common assumptions, private Chinese firms, not SOEs or wealthy individuals, are the top investors in commercial property. The Pacific United States receives a sizable share of this investment, with property deals in Los Angeles, San Francisco, and Hawaii alone adding up to $588 million during the first three quarters of 2014.[29] Some of the higher-profile investments in recent years, though, have been on the East Coast. In New York City, Chinese investments include:

- Fosun's October 2013 purchase of Chase Manhattan Plaza ($725 million);[30]

- The May 2013 acquisition of a stake in the General Motors building by a conglomerate of Chinese investors ($700 million);[31]

- Greenland Group's June 2014 buy-in to the Pacific Park project (formerly Atlantic Yards) in Brooklyn (total project value $5 billion);[32]

- The October 2014 sale of the Waldorf Astoria to China's Anbang Insurance Group ($1.95 billion);[33] and

- Bank of China's planned 2015 purchase of 7 Bryant Park ($600 million).[34]

According to industry professionals, the acquisition of stabilized assets like office buildings and hotels that require a longer-term commitment for rental incomes are seen as a "toe in the water"—a gauge for the market, a way to become familiar with the local tax system, and a basis for further development. This is especially true of Chinese developers investing in U.S. properties, many of whom seek to better understand local markets before investing in a greenfield project. In some cases, after the initial purchase has been made and some rental income has been

---

* According to Cushman & Wakefield, the United States received nearly $10 billion in Chinese outbound real estate investment between 2008 and June 2014. The United Kingdom ranked a distant second (nearly $6 billion). Cushman & Wakefield, *China's Outbound Boom: The Rise of Chinese Investment in Global Real Estate* (October 2014), pp. 3, 10.

† A greenfield investment is a form of FDI where a parent company starts a new venture in a foreign country by constructing new operational facilities from the ground up. In addition to building new facilities, most parent companies also create new long-term jobs in the foreign country by hiring new employees. Investopedia, "Green Field Investment." *http://www.investopedia.com/terms/g/greenfield.asp.*

‡ Rhodium Group classifies as "private" those companies that have 80 percent or more private ownership.

generated, Chinese developers may use office buildings acquired previously as a base for future expansion.[35] Dalian Wanda Group, a private conglomerate that acquired the U.S. movie theater chain AMC for $2.6 billion in May 2012, has been particularly successful in this respect.[36] Its future commercial developments could combine leasing of office and retail space with new AMC movie theaters.

Chinese insurance companies, a distinct group from developers, are also interested in acquiring stabilized assets like office buildings and other nonresidential rental properties. Both private and state-owned insurance companies have been restricted from buying stabilized assets in the domestic market, resulting in increased interest in long-hold properties abroad. For privately owned insurance companies, these investments are seen as a supplement to domestic property holdings and as a way to diversify overall assets—an essential strategy in a market dominated by large, state-owned firms. In 2012, the China Insurance Regulatory Commission (CIRC) allowed Chinese insurers to invest a higher percentage of their portfolios in real estate, a move that could stimulate overseas investment as well. However, supplementing this expansion, CIRC in February 2014 announced a cap on "real estate category assets" at 30 percent of total investments.[37] The cap suggests wariness by CIRC about poorly allocated investment in illiquid property assets, which could do lasting damage to the balance sheets of insurance companies.

The nature and extent of Chinese real estate investment varies across the United States. Over the last decade, Chinese investors have focused on large "gateway cities" such as San Francisco, Los Angeles, and New York, where assets are pricier but also easier to evaluate and access. In 2014, Chinese investment in New York totaled over $6.7 billion, with the majority of deals in Manhattan. California had the second-highest total investment in 2014, with more than $1.6 billion, the majority in Los Angeles ($793 million) and San Francisco ($558 million).[38] Recently, there has been greater geographic dispersion as Chinese companies seek properties that suit their individual and commercial needs, which may go beyond simple portfolio returns.[39] Second- and third-tier cities could become a common destination for Chinese capital as well, though this diversification is in its early stages.[40]

In many U.S. states, there is a gap between the way the state office operates and the way Chinese companies seek investment opportunities. What potential investors often look for is a comprehensive list of the investment opportunities available in a state or region. What states tend to lack is a centralized plan for how to respond to such investment inquiries and "close the deals."[41] Some state officials have begun to think about presenting investment opportunities to Chinese investors in a different way—for instance, with a catalogue that lists properties available for sale in their state.[42] Bradley Gillenwater, regional manager for Asia at the Maryland Department of Business and Economic Development, stated:

> What [the Chinese] want is basically a list of investments that are kind of teed up and ready to go, so that a Chinese national or company can key into it. It typically just doesn't operate that way in the United States, but they want to see it duplicated because that's what they do. I'm sure you've seen these books that the various provinces and municipalities [in China] have.[43]

According to a New Jersey official, many Chinese property developers are under the impression that once political support is secured from local officials, they can just start building, unaware of the detailed permitting work required.[44] Experts at Cushman & Wakefield, a commercial real estate brokerage firm, noted small Chinese investors looking to the United States are often unprepared for the degree of complexity involved in seeing a real estate deal through from start to finish. A redeeming quality of Chinese investors, however, is their patience. Initial investments that go sour are often treated as a learning experience. Unlike short-term investors in the United States, well-capitalized investors from China can afford to wait for a profit.[45]

Individual Investments in Residential and Small-Scale Properties

Chinese individuals are pouring money into U.S. residential and small-scale commercial properties. This is especially evident in suburban centers near major universities. Industry professionals interviewed by Commission staff said even areas with high median property values—like suburban Los Angeles—are popular with Chinese investors looking for a second home.[46] There is a marked preference for homes in California, likely due to the state's well-networked Chinese community, diversified economy, and elite academic institutions.[47]

A 2014 report by the National Realtors' Association sheds light on the preferences of foreign nationals who purchase homes in the United States (see Table 1).[48] The report illustrates that most Chinese buyers are wealthy individuals who regard the acquired property primarily as an investment:

- Three-quarters of Chinese buyers pay all cash.

- Nearly half of Chinese nationals plan to use the acquired residence for less than six months a year.

- Only two-fifths of Chinese nationals plan to make their U.S. home a primary residence.

Table 1: Preferences of Home Buyers in the United States: Indian, Chinese, and UK Nationals

Photo Removed Due to Copyright Restrictions

Source: Lawrence Yun, Jed Smith, and Gay Cororaton, *2014 Profile of International Home Buying Activity* (National Association of Realtors, June 2014).

By buying homes chiefly for investment purposes, Chinese buyers may exacerbate housing bubbles. In San Francisco, for example, real estate cycles take about five to seven years to run their course. The current surge in prices, only three years old, could persist for quite some time, make housing less affordable for local residents.[49]

A likely "push" factor for Chinese buyers is the cooling down of China's domestic property market. Wary of asset bubbles, the Chinese government has sought to curb speculative investment, issuing new rules forcing developers to apply for presale permits and requiring exorbitant down payments of up to half of the purchase price.[50] Experts at Cushman & Wakefield told Commission staff:

One of the big problems that we have [regarding the expectations of Chinese investors] is that people are not used to the price dropping. The price of real estate has been going up for so long that if a Chinese person buys a property and the next day the price gets slashed, the buyer thinks that was the developer's fault, not theirs, for paying too much.[51]

While China's property market could rebound from its cyclical slump, structural factors are also influencing capital flight from the Mainland. A 2014 survey by the Shanghai research firm Hurun showed 64 percent of Chinese individuals with assets of more than $1.6 million were either emigrating or planning to do so. Driving this trend are concerns about pollution, lax food safety, and other quality of life factors.[*] China's well-connected elite is already transferring considerable wealth offshore. Using data obtained from foreign tax havens, the International Consortium of Investigative Journalists reported in January 2014 that 22,000 clients of offshore financial institutions had addresses in mainland China and Hong Kong.[52] The report, censored in mainland China, included some of China's most powerful men and women—including at least 15 of the richest members of the National People's Congress and executives from state-owned companies entangled in corruption scandals.[53]

An October 2014 report by *Businessweek* illustrates the extent to which wealthy, well-connected Chinese are buying homes in Arcadia, a suburban community near Los Angeles. Among the homeowners is the wife of Chen Qingbo. Mr. Chen is one of China's wealthiest individuals and was arrested by Chinese officials for investor fraud in June of last year. Also owning homes in Arcadia are the wife of Cheng Qingbo's brother Cheng Qingtao, who owns a majority stake in one of China's oldest SOEs, China Huayang Economic & Trade Group; the wife of Du Jianming, the largest private builder of steel structures in China; and Tao Weisheng, a Chongqing hotel developer who in 2004 paid a Chinese Communist Party official's gambling debt in Macau.[54]

China allows individuals to transfer only $50,000 out of the country each year.[55] But wealthy Chinese individuals can resort to various means to circumvent these capital controls. It is perfectly legal to maintain personal and business accounts in Hong Kong, where there are no capital restrictions. International banks such as HSBC also help China-based clients take out loans in the United States.[56] A riskier tactic is to directly forego controls on the Mainland. False invoicing of export and import receipts has become rampant in recent years.[57][†] China's 2013 decision to relax the capital requirement for new businesses could also open avenues for wealthy individuals to move funds out of the country via small businesses.[58]

Chinese Investors and the EB-5 Visa Program

The Influx of Chinese EB-5 Applicants

Started 24 years ago, the U.S. EB-5 immigrant investor visa allows foreign nationals and their family members to receive a conditional green card in exchange for an investment of $500,000 in geographic areas of the United States that have high unemployment rates, or $1 million in other areas. The EB-5 provides wealthy Chinese and their families a dual benefit: they can obtain permission to work and reside in the United States while diversifying their wealth into U.S. commercial property and other assets. The EB-5 program allots 10,000 visas annually, and there is an existing cap on the number of visas from each country. If other countries do not reach the cap, however, Chinese applicants can fill these spots.[59]

Initially envisioned as a program to attract investors from around the world, the EB-5 program has recently been flooded by wealthy Chinese nationals. China hit its annual cap for the first time in 2013, as the number of visas issued to Chinese citizens reached 6,895 (versus less than 2,500 in 2011). Chinese nationals that year accounted for 80 percent of total EB-5 visas issued (versus 14 percent in 2007).[60] Through August 2014, China's share increased further, to 85 percent.[61] The State Department subsequently announced that EB-5 visas would be "unavailable" to Chinese individuals until the 2015 fiscal year—the first time this occurred in the program's history.[62]

U.S. states have also registered a surge in EB-5 requests and questions in the last few years. Some officials have not been particularly excited by the prospect. An Arkansas official stated Chinese investors are presently more

---

[*] For more information on China's quality of life concerns, see U.S.-China Economic and Security Review Commission, *2013 Annual Report to Congress*, November 2013 Chapter 1.4 and *2014 Annual Report to Congress*, November 2014, Chapter 1.3 and 2.3. These reports can be accessed at *http://www.uscc.gov*.

[†] For more information on China's illicit capital outflows through Macau, see U.S.-China Economic and Security Review Commission, *2013 Annual Report to Congress*, November 2013, Chapter 3.3. This report can be accessed at *http://www.uscc.gov*.

interested in EB-5 visas than in setting up a manufacturing facility in her state.[63] A representative from Georgia, a state that aggressively courts Chinese investors, said the China office does not actively promote EB-5 programs.[64] South Carolina's China office appears to take a similar approach.[65]

Other states, by contrast, are quite enthusiastic. An official in Pennsylvania said his state was one of the first to introduce the EB-5 program, and claimed the program facilitated a $100 million investment in Philadelphia's Comcast Tower.[66] In Rockford, Illinois, 92 EB-5 investors, mostly from China, are joining hands with billionaire investor Warren Buffet to remodel a skyscraper in conjunction with a local urban renewal program.[67] Meanwhile, the state of Michigan plans to use advertisements for EB-5 visas to attract Chinese tourists.[68]

There is an incentive not to screen Chinese EB-5 investors too rigorously. They can fill an important gap by investing in underdeveloped areas that domestic investors avoid. They also benefit private property developers— according to *Forbes*, the cost of EB-5 capital runs between 4 percent and 6 percent a year—less than half of what developers would typically have to pay for mezzanine debt or to equity investors.[69] But the EB-5 program presents real risks. These revolve around the proliferation of privately run Immigrant Investor Regional Centers ("Regional Centers"), the loose designation of EB-5 Investor Targeted Employment Areas (TEAs), and the lack of safeguards against fraudulent behavior.

Immigrant Investor Regional Centers

Immigrant Investor Regional Centers ("Regional Centers") play an important role in administering the EB-5 program at the local level. Although EB-5 investors can act on their own, they often turn to Regional Centers to help identify and vet projects that qualify for the EB-5 program, and to seek assistance with domestic and international compliance work. Regional Centers are maintained by private individuals or companies for their own profit. The business can be very lucrative: a California official revealed that a San Francisco-based Regional Center, one of the state's largest, has attracted cumulative investment of $825 million, mostly from China.[70]

Research by Commission staff shows that virtually all U.S. states have Regional Centers. The distribution by state roughly correlates with each state's contribution to the national economy (see Figure 2). There are important outliers, however. California, with 155 Regional Centers, accounts for nearly one in five centers nationwide. Florida, Nevada, and Washington are also home to a disproportionate number.[71]

U.S. Citizenship and Immigration Services (USCIS) defines a Regional Center as "any economic unit, public or private, engaged in the promotion of economic growth, improved regional productivity, job creation and increased domestic capital investment."[72] As of February 2, 2015, USCIS had approved 630 Regional Centers. Regional centers can operate in multiple states and thus be listed in more than one state (resulting in 848 total entries in the USCIS database). Although the centers require approval from USCIS, the federal agency cautions that its approvals do not "constitute USCIS endorsement of the activities of that Regional Center," "guarantee compliance with U.S. securities laws," or "minimize or eliminate risk to the investor." The agency encourages potential investors to "seek professional advice when making any investment decisions."[73]

Foreign investors are prone to mistaking the privately operated Regional Centers for government-sponsored areas vetted for development.[74] Licensed Regional Centers, often for-profit operations independent of state governments, are zoned strategically to make maximum use of potential investment and to cater to the needs of visa seekers. A host of less than trustworthy companies and consultancies, exploiting a lack of regulatory oversight, have claimed experience in the EB-5 realm where none exists.[75] Abigail Browning, who is closely involved with EB-5 regulation at the California governor's office, told Commission staff the state government has little authority when it comes to regulating Regional Centers:

> I don't think [the Regional Center approval process] is rigorous at all. You just need to have a banker, a lawyer, and somebody else get together and there you go....There is no way for us [as the state government] to go in there and say "this Regional Center is legitimate, this one is not, this one's a scam," because it is a liability issue and if [the federal government] is not willing to do it, we're certainly not going to be willing to do it....We don't want California to have a bad name for attracting investment. However, there is nothing really we can do about [a problem] until it actually happens. It is a federal program and we have to keep our distance.[76]

Figure 2: U.S. States' Share of Immigrant Investor Regional Centers and National GDP (Share % of 821 Regional Centers nationwide)

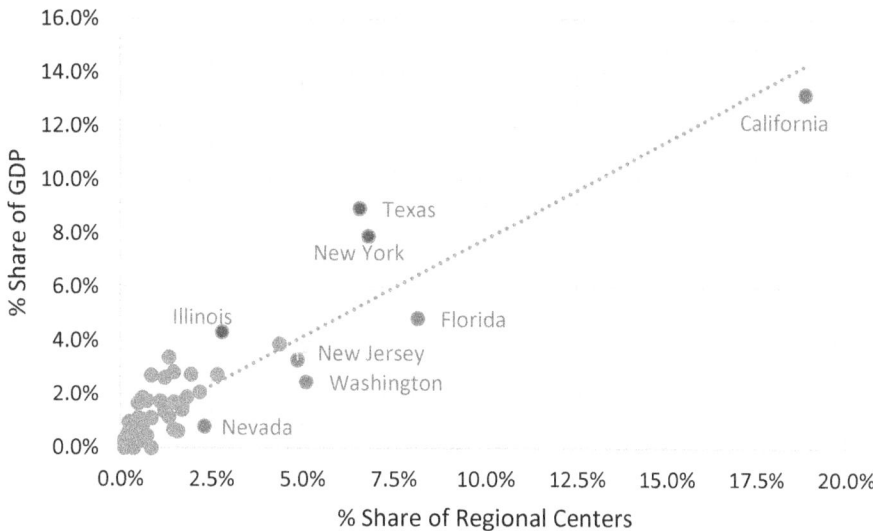

Sources: Stats America; U.S. Citizenship and Immigration Services.
Note 1: Dots in red and black are for important outliers. States in black have a smaller share of Regional Centers than GDP; states in red have more.
Note 2: Sample includes all 50 states. R-squared is .825.
Note 3: There are a total of 14 Regional Centers in Guam, Puerto Rico, the Virgin Islands, and the Mariam Islands, for which GDP data was not available.
Note 4: GDP is based on gross state product (GSP) for 2013.

In an attempt to keep a tab on the activities of Regional Centers, the California governor's office asks these entities to fill out an annual voluntary survey that records how much business they have done and with whom, along with documents to corroborate the facts. The incentive to fill out the survey is that the state government openly endorses the Regional Centers that comply, which should make it easier for them to attract business. Still, only dozen or so Regional Centers responded to California's voluntary survey last year.[77] This raises the possibility that certain Regional Centers exist only on paper, wish to disguise their poor performance, or have reason not to disclose how they do business.

Targeted Employment Areas

Regional Centers assist immigrant investors in filing for the designation of TEAs with state authorities. TEAs are defined as areas that have experienced an unemployment rate at least 150 percent above the national average. Chinese nationals who invest in TEAs need only commit $500,000 to obtain an EB-5 visa, compared to $1 million in non-TEA regions.[78] According to Ms. Browning, $1 million investments are rare, since it is easier to invest half as much and incur the compliance costs of TEA certification.[79]

Unlike the federal approval required for Regional Centers, certification of TEAs in California rests with the state government. (The state's TEA approval letter is submitted to USCIS as part of the EB-5 application.) Ms. Browning said her office received 689 TEA applications in 2014 alone, compared with 389 in 2013.[80] In the first four weeks of 2015, the state received 61 new applications, on pace for 732 by the end of this year.[81] The majority of applicants, she said, had Chinese names.[82]

Applicants often draw up artificially large TEAs in order to incorporate low-income, high-unemployment areas within the bounds of an investment project. One such example, from the Chicago O'Hare project, stretched over eight miles around the airport and Chicago suburbs to meet the EB-5 requirements for registered unemployment.[83]

Ms. Browning told Commission staff that since responsibility for TEA certification was shifted to her office in 2012, the process has become more standardized in California. Ms. Browning uses unemployment data from U.S. Census tracts as the baseline for assessing TEA zones; the exception is a special TEA, which allows applicants to incorporate up to 12 contiguous Census tracts.[84] The argument is that those employed at the EB-5 investor's new business in one tract could commute there from another.[85] However, the barrier to getting TEA certification is still fairly low, as high-unemployment areas can be identified even in super-wealthy counties. Browning stated:

> *Even though there are some very high employment areas in California, it is very hard to find something that doesn't qualify. It amazes me now and then because the way we have it broken down with Census tracts, I've qualified things that are in the middle of Beverly Hills. You'd think that that wouldn't be a high unemployment area.*[86]

The EB-5 program's requirement that a proposed investment create a minimum of ten full-time jobs has also come under suspicion, since the nature and duration requirement of such jobs is not clear from the regulations, and the government's ability to monitor and enforce this provision is limited. In California, Ms. Browning attempts to counteract this problem by requiring TEA applicants to notify their project to county- or city-level governments.[87] This helps ensure the job creation claims are realistic, puts the project on the radar of local officials, and allows state officials to verify whether the investor is indeed creating the jobs pledged. Nonetheless, such measures are of an informal nature, since the official paperwork is filed with USCIS at the federal level.[88]

Investor Fraud

An imminent risk concerning the EB-5 program is outright investor fraud. Mr. Gillenwater, an investment promotion official in Maryland, told Commission staff:

> *There are people in China claiming they are from one of these federally approved Regional Centers and saying, "Hey, I have this escrow account set up. You, a Chinese investor, if you provide me some money now and end up not getting your green card, you'll get your money back." And you know what some of these people are doing with that money—they disappear.... It's pretty easy to just forge a document and give it to someone and say, "Here, look, this is a letter that confirms that I am one of these EB-5 Regional Centers. It's not listed on the website right now but it'll be up any day now."*[89]

Two troubled projects in particular, one outside of Chicago in the shadow of O'Hare airport and the other in South Dakota, have come to light:

- In Chicago, a "developer" hoping to build a $912 million hotel and convention complex was indicted in August 2014 on federal fraud charges for duping some 290 Chinese investors. The complex, marketed as a state-of-the-art convention center, was never started. The father-son team behind the project not only had no development experience, but also vastly overstated the amount of funding they had secured from federal and state sources, in an attempt to grease the project into success.[90]

- In South Dakota, a state official committed suicide after he was placed under investigation for the mismanagement and fraudulent allocation of funds secured through the EB-5 program, as well as a portion of state funds that had been offered as a matching investment. The case is still under investigation and the EB-5 program has since shut down in South Dakota.[91]

Such questionable tactics raise questions about the benefits of the program and whether foreign investors, often disinclined or unable to assess business risks, are adding the intended value to the U.S. economy.[92]

A Sample of Chinese Investment in U.S. Industry

Light Manufacturing

Stable and cheap energy prices are an important driver of Chinese investment into the United States. A specific beneficiary is the petrochemical industry:

- In Laurens County, South Carolina, China's Uniscite Inc., a chemical producer, agreed in February 2012 to invest $77 million in a new facility to produce high-quality, biaxially oriented polypropylene (BOPP) film, a plastic used in a wide variety of food packaging. The plant became operational in 2014. The project is expected to create 120 direct jobs.[93]

- In St. James Parish, Louisiana, Wang Jinshu, the Communist Party Secretary for the northeastern Chinese village of Yuhuang and a delegate to the National People's Congress, is heading a $1.85 billion investment in a methanol plant, to be built in 2015–2016. According to a news report, the investment comes with a $9.5 million incentive package from the state of Louisiana.[94] Local economic development authorities told the news outlet Al Jazeera that "St. James Parish is an ideal location for the methanol plant because of readily accessible deep water and cheap fuel from the shale oil boom that will help cut production costs."[95]

- Further north, in Pennsylvania, the heartland of the U.S. shale boom, Chinese plastics manufacturer Fuling Plastics has created 75 jobs with a new facility in Allentown.[96]

Another emerging segment for Chinese light manufacturing investment is textiles. China's 2001 accession to the World Trade Organization (WTO) proved detrimental to U.S. domestic textile production. U.S. cotton growers have since shifted their sales from U.S. clothing makers to Chinese producers.* Today, however, some Asian textile manufacturers are setting up production in the southeastern United States.

Among them is Keer Group Co., a medium-sized enterprise from Hangzhou, a textile center in China's Zhejiang province. The company has agreed to invest $218 million to build a factory in Lancaster County, South Carolina, in the vicinity of large cotton plantations. John Ling, who heads South Carolina's representative office in China, was instrumental in bringing Keer to his state. On a recent visit to Lancaster, he was astonished to see that Keer had already completed its first 250,000-square-foot building and was planning another building of the same size to be built in 2015. He said Keer is creating 501 direct jobs with its project.[97]

Several factors influenced Keer's decision. CEO Zhu Shanqing claims his company will pay only half as much for electricity in Lancaster County as in Hangzhou, which will help offset the difference in labor costs.[98] The preferential "yarn forward rule" the United States maintains with its free trade partners in Central America is another plus: Keer can ship yarn from the United States to manufacturers in Central America, who then send the finished clothes duty-free back to the United States, a privilege not accorded to Chinese exporters on the Mainland.[99]

Keer may also be responding to market-distorting policies enacted by the Chinese government. In the past, Beijing has supported Chinese textile producers by means of an undervalued currency and other export incentives. But beginning in 2011, the government instituted a policy of procuring cotton into national reserves, paying above world prices in order to support domestic growers. As a result, cotton became more expensive in China than on the world market, pinching China's low-margin textile sector. The yarn industry has responded by importing cheaper cotton from abroad in excess of China's WTO tariff-rate quota, even though this involves high import tariffs. Keer has pursued an alternative strategy, venturing abroad to produce yarn directly at the site of cotton production.[100]

Investing in the United States to circumvent trade barriers is becoming a pattern among Chinese manufacturers. Dennis Pruitt, an investment promotion official at the Missouri Partnership, told Commission staff that Chinese

---

* Mark Lange, chief executive officer (CEO) of the National Cotton Council, told the Commission at a 2013 hearing that between 2001 and 2009, the cotton used in China's textile industry increased from 20 million bales to 50 million bales, while the U.S. use of cotton dropped from 11 million to four million bales. By 2013, U.S. cotton producers shipped half of their crop to China, and the U.S. textile workforce was only one-fourth as large as two decades earlier. U.S.-China Economic and Security Review Commission, *Hearing on China's Agriculture Policy and U.S. Access to China's Market*, testimony of Mark Lange, April 25, 2013.

solar panel manufacturers are beginning to seek manufacturing opportunities in his state.[101] His guess is that these companies are responding not only to rising U.S. demand for solar energy, but also to U.S. antidumping (AD) duties on China-origin panels.[102] Imposed by the U.S. Department of Commerce (DOC) in 2012, the duties were subject to evasion initially, as Chinese panel makers resorted to sourcing solar cells from Taiwan and other third countries. The DOC modified the duties in December 2014 to close this loophole.[103]

Food and Tobacco

Chinese companies are also availing themselves of opportunities in the U.S. food and tobacco sectors. The most high-profile deal was Shuanghui's 2013 acquisition of Smithfield Group, the world's largest pork producer. The acquisition provides Shuanghui with access to premium U.S. pork products and advanced industry farming techniques and technology, at a time when food safety is preoccupying Chinese consumers.* According to a North Carolina official, the acquisition caused some apprehension in her state about job shedding, since one of Smithfield's main slaughtering plants is based in North Carolina.[104] But she maintained these concerns had died down by the summer of 2014, as Shuanghui had not shut down or downsized the Smithfield facilities.[105]

While Shuanghui entered North Carolina indirectly through a takeover deal, China's state-owned tobacco products company, China Tobacco, opened an office in the state in 2013. According to Peter Thornton, assistant director for international marketing with the North Carolina Department of Agriculture and Consumer Services, the office is expected to serve as the base for China Tobacco's North American leaf-buying operation for cigarette manufacturing.[106] While China Tobacco's local office is small, the state expects it will make significant buys of North Carolina tobacco.[107]

Figure 3: U.S. Tobacco Exports and the Share of Japan and China
(Metric tons thousands; share %)

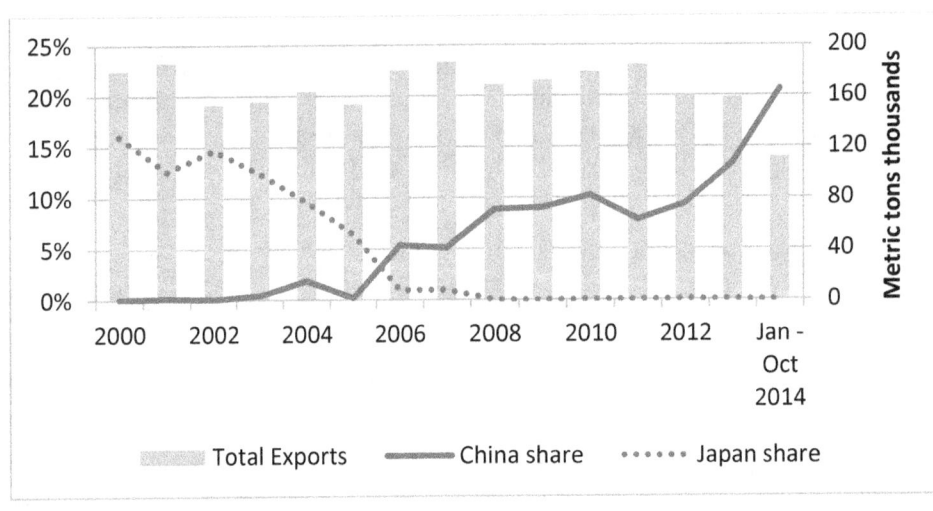

Source: U.S. Department of Agriculture.

North Carolina state officials were pivotal in bringing China Tobacco to their state. North Carolina Agriculture Commissioner Steve Troxler led trade missions to China in 2009 and 2011, and his department opened its own trade office in Beijing in 2011.[108] At the opening ceremony of the China Tobacco office, Liang Zhanhua, the president of the new subsidiary, claimed several U.S. states had tried to convince China Tobacco to set up operations in their state. Ultimately, North Carolina was chosen due to its proximity to tobacco farming and to the "tremendous help" the company received from North Carolina officials.[109]

---

* For more information, see the June 2013 edition of the *USCC Monthly Trade Bulletin*. The report can be accessed at *http://www.uscc.gov*.

World Health Organization figures show nearly two-thirds of Chinese men smoke, constituting the largest tobacco-consuming population in the world.[110] The decline of smoking in the United States, in turn, has left U.S. tobacco growers seeking new markets, not least in North Carolina, the leading tobacco-growing state. Data from the U.S. Department of Agriculture show U.S. tobacco exports have declined in recent years, but the share of U.S. tobacco going to China has increased (see Figure 3 on previous page). China Tobacco, a national monopoly with political clout, seeks to raise profits by marketing premium brands that use U.S. tobacco.

An unusual case of Chinese agriculture investment is the fishery industry in the U.S. Midwest. Asian carp are invading the Mississippi River and other major waterways, causing damage to native fish populations because they outcompete other fish for food and space.[111] According to Mr. Pruitt, the Missouri official, four Chinese companies have approached his office seeking investment in Asian carp processing. He explained:

> *Asian carp is a popular dish in China. Some companies are looking at ways to flash-freeze dry these fish and ship them over to China. You have other Chinese investors that are saying, "Look, we can come over here and use the fish for fertilizer. We can extract some of the oils from the fish for pharmaceutical products...." What we've been doing is trying to propose meetings between Chinese investors and fishermen in Missouri, and ultimately come to a discussion about where to build this plant....Given the confluence of the two biggest rivers in the United States [here], the Missouri and the Mississippi, it makes sense for Chinese companies to come over and look at solving the Asian carp problem. Sometimes these are companies or investors that aren't necessarily fish processing companies. They are entrepreneurs that have been successful in China; one I've dealt with is a metal machine company and is not food-related. But they see an opportunity due to the Chinese desire for Asian carp and the government policy at the state level to eradicate Asian carp in the Midwest.[112]*

The Automotive Sector

China today produces more automobiles than any other country. U.S. auto companies attempting to export to China or to create profitable investments there face considerable obstacles, including Chinese government ownership over key producers, discriminatory government procurement policies, high import tariffs, restrictions on foreign majority ownership of China-based auto production, and the requirement that all foreign automotive manufacturers in China engage in joint ventures with Chinese partners.* Earlier this year, a WTO panel sided with the United States in a dispute over China's punitive tariffs on $5 billion worth of U.S. large-engine vehicles.[113]

At the same time, China is becoming the most dynamic growth market for U.S.-branded vehicle makers. In 2014, China ranked among the top destinations for U.S. passenger car exports, second only to Canada.[114] General Motors and Ford Motor Co. are expanding their production capacity in North America as well as China.†

China is also emerging as an important investor in the U.S. automotive industry. Among the first companies to arrive was the auto parts maker Wanxiang Group, which set up a U.S. subsidiary in 1994 and proceeded to purchase a number of small auto parts companies in the Midwest.[115] In January 2014, Wanxiang won a bid to acquire California-based Fisker Automotive, which had reduced its workforce by 75 percent and filed for Chapter 11 bankruptcy. As part of its bid, Wanxiang insisted that Fisker revive production of its hybrid car model, Karma.[116] According to Gordon G. Chang, a prominent commentator on China's economy, Wanxiang's plan is to challenge U.S.-based Tesla Motors in the electric car segment.[117]

Yanfeng USA Automotive Trim Systems, a Michigan-based subsidiary of Yanfeng Visteon of China, supplies parts to companies such as General Motors and Chrysler. In April 2013, it announced a $45 million investment in a greenfield plant in Missouri. According to data obtained by Commission staff from Mr. Pruitt, the deal added to a list of 40 investment projects in the Missouri auto industry since 2011.[118] At a ceremony commemorating the investment, Missouri Governor Jay Nixon stated:

---

* For more information, see U.S.-China Economic and Security Review Commission, *2006 Annual Report to Congress*, November 2006, Chapter 4. This report can be accessed at *http://www.uscc.gov*.

† For more information, see Iacob Koch-Weser, *China's Hunger for U.S. Planes and Cars: Assessing the Risks* (U.S.-China Economic and Security Review Commission, March 27, 2014). This report can be accessed at *http://www.uscc.gov*.

The historic expansions by Ford and General Motors during 2011 have transformed Missouri's economy, putting our state on the map as the leader of the rebirth of the American auto industry...Yanfeng's decision to build a new production facility in Riverside and create 263 new manufacturing jobs is more excellent news for our state's automotive industry sector and economy as a whole. "[119]

An official at the Michigan Economic Development Corporation told Commission staff that Chinese auto investments are playing a significant role in his state's economic development. He estimated that the acquisition of parts maker Nexteer by Pacific Century Motors in November 2010 has saved 2,500 jobs and added 1,000 new jobs since 2010.[120] While Michigan became a right-to-work state* in 2013, the employees at Nexteer are members of the United Auto Workers (UAW) union. According to the official, UAW came to Nexteer after the Chinese acquisition with an offer to make significant wage concessions, ultimately opting for a two-tier wage system in which new employees start at a lower wage rate.[121]

At the time of the Nexteer acquisition, Pacific Century Motors was a subsidiary of E-town, the Beijing municipal government's investment company, and Tempo Group, a Chinese car component manufacturer.[122] In March 2011, AVIC Automobile Industry Holding Co., one of China's largest state-owned auto parts manufacturers, purchased a 51 percent majority interest in Pacific Century Motors. As a result, Nexteer is now effectively owned by a Chinese SOE.[123]

Also important for Michigan has been the arrival of Shanghai Automotive Investment Corporation (SAIC), a central government SOE and the largest auto maker in China. SAIC over the last five years has set up extensive manufacturing operations in the state, primarily auto parts subsidiaries, and also moved its North American headquarters there from California.[124]

Transport Infrastructure

There is a pressing need to upgrade U.S. transport infrastructure. The 2007 collapse of the I-35W Mississippi River Bridge in Minneapolis, Minnesota served as a wakeup call to local officials. To optimize fiscal spending, state and municipal governments have turned to foreign and private companies as sources of investment capital and cheap equipment.

China is figuring into these plans. In October 2014, for example, China CNR Corp. signed an agreement with the Boston transportation authority to provide 284 cars to the Boston subway, with an option for 58 more. The deal is worth $567 million.[125] CNR Corp., a central state-owned manufacturer of rolling stock and train cars, has profited from supplying China's high-speed rail projects. Around the time of the Boston deal, CNR entered talks with CSR Corp., a rival Chinese train maker, to merge into one large company capable of competing with the likes of Siemens and Bombardier.[126] Deals like the one in Boston could incentivize CNR and CSR to establish a long-term presence in the U.S. market.

Whether or not to procure materials from China for U.S. construction projects has been a subject of contention. In June 2012, for example, the Alliance for American Manufacturing sponsored a billboard campaign criticizing the use of China-origin steel for the San Francisco-Oakland Bay Bridge. The central tower and the two 1,500-foot steel road decks were fabricated in a specially built factory in China and shipped to San Francisco Bay. The decision to source from China was made by the California Department of Transportation.[127]

According to Mr. Gillenwater, the state of Maryland has sought foreign investment in transport infrastructure, with corresponding interest from the U.S. Chamber of Commerce in getting Chinese investors involved.[128] Three years ago, ahead of contract bidding for extensions of the red and purple lines of the Washington Metropolitan Area Transit Authority Metrorail, several memoranda of understanding were signed with Chinese companies. There was a "good deal of interest" from China Construction America, the New York-based subsidiary of a large Chinese SOE, which was already doing smaller construction projects throughout the United States.† China Export-Import

---

* A Right to Work law secures the right of employees to decide for themselves whether to join or financially support a union. At present, 24 U.S. states, concentrated in the U.S. South, have right-to-work laws. Legal Defense Foundation Inc., "Right to Work States." *http://www.nrtw.org/rtws.htm.*

† For more information, see China Construction America, "Projects." *http://www.chinaconstruction.us/Project1.jsp.*

Bank also showed interest, presumably to incentivize exports of construction materials from China. Ultimately, however, no Chinese companies submitted bids to build the DC Metrorail lines.[129]

In January this year, the state of California began construction on a $68 billion high-speed rail system.[130] Governor Jerry Brown has studied China's extensive high-speed rail system and is using it as a way to promote his own plan. The governor has taken a ride on the Shanghai-Beijing high-speed rail line, accompanied by the chairman of California's high-speed rail board, Dan Richard.[131] However, some reports suggest costs for the California project have soared. Major construction, originally slated to start at the end of 2012, has experienced delays. Officials in charge of the project still claim they can complete it on budget and meet a 2017 deadline for the use of federal construction grants on the initial section of track.[132]

Healthcare and Pharmaceuticals

Chinese investors are also making inroads into higher value-added segments of the U.S. economy. An example is healthcare and pharmaceuticals, an industry of strategic importance to China as its population ages and noncommunicable diseases proliferate.* In 2008, Beijing-based JOINN Laboratories set up a U.S. branch in Germantown, Maryland, close to the U.S. Food and Drug Administration and the National Institutes of Health. Established in 1995, with headquarters in Beijing, JOINN was the first privately held preclinical drug discovery and development contract research organization in China. The Maryland subsidiary office deals mainly with global drug application filings.[133]

JOINN is also a flagship Chinese investor in California. In its April 2013 press release announcing the creation of a China representative office, the California governor's office reported that JOINN is committing $50 million to set up a pharmaceutical production plant in cooperation with Staidson Pharmaceuticals. The plant will be located in Richmond at the former manufacturing facility of Bayer AG, a German pharmaceutical company.[134]

In Maryland, JOINN is only one of several healthcare-related investors from China. Mr. Gillenwater claimed half of the 19 Chinese companies in his state are engaged in the biopharmaceuticals, healthcare, and medical device fields.[135] In the summer of 2014, Tasly Group, a biopharmaceutical company from Tianjin, established a new subsidiary in Rockville, commemorated by a ribbon-cutting ceremony attended by Mr. Gillenwater. Tasly has a traditional Chinese medicine (TCM) drug now in Phase 3 of clinical trials that it wants to market in the United States. To date, no TCM drug has ever passed Phase 3 trials and been sold in the United States.[136]

Investment Promotion Strategies of U.S. States

Variation in State Strategies

Based on information compiled by Commission staff from state government websites, 25 U.S. states currently have representative offices in China. States with China offices cluster in certain regions, notably the Southeast, the Far West, and the central United States (see Figure 4). For the most part, states in the Rocky Mountains, the Southwest, and New England have not established a presence in China. By the same token, only certain U.S. states and local authorities are members of the Council of American States in China (CASIC), an organization that promotes bilateral economic exchanges.†

---

* For more information, see U.S.-China Economic and Security Review Commission, *2014 Annual Report to Congress*, November 2014, Chapter 1.3. This report can be accessed at *http://www.uscc.gov.*

† CASIC brings together the representative offices of U.S. states, cities, tourism authorities, and ports located in China to better serve the overall mission of U.S. state offices in China. CASIC's primary objective is to serve as a bridge to promote trade, tourism, logistics, education, and investment between the United States and China. One of its main activities is to organize U.S. pavilions at major trade shows and investment events of interest to CASIC members, and to facilitate strong working relationships with other trade organizations, chambers of commerce, and Chinese government agencies. Council of American States in China, "About CASIC." *http://www.casic.us/about.asp?cd=2.*

There is some correlation between the amount of Chinese investment U.S. states receive and their presence in China (see Figure 5). There are exceptions, however. Texas, Colorado, and Oklahoma are major recipients of Chinese investments but have no China presence. Arkansas and Mississippi have a China presence, but the value of Chinese investment in their states is relatively small.

Figure 4: U.S. States with Representative Offices in China
(States with offices in China marked in yellow)

Source: Compiled from information on state government websites.

Figure 5: Cumulative Chinese Investment by U.S. State, 2000–Q3 2014
(Darker color = higher value of deals; numbers indicate number of deals)

Photo Removed Due to Copyright Restrictions

Source: Rhodium Group, "China Investment Monitor." http://rhg.com/interactive/china-investment-monitor.

U.S. states accord different levels of priority to promotional work in China. States from the U.S. South tend to conduct aggressive outreach. Georgia has had continuous representation in China since 2007, and is among a few states with two separate offices on the Mainland: an investment promotion office in Qingdao and a trade office in Shanghai, each with two staff. The state promotes investment in a wide range of manufacturing industries. Its successes so far include a $60 million greenfield plant by Sany, China's largest machinery maker, and a $10 million investment by the aviation information technology (IT) company Travel Sky.[137]

In China since April 2005, South Carolina has only one representative in China but is also doing substantial outreach work among medium-sized Chinese manufacturers. Mr. Ling reported that his office has landed at least three meaningful investment projects so far (yarn making, industrial fiber, and chemicals) with a combined value of $340 million.[138] Mr. Ling prefers a "long-term and committed approach": He accompanies Chinese companies on visits to South Carolina, and works with many of them years after they establish their South Carolina operations.[139] He claimed demand for his office's services has increased substantially, from three to four prospective companies each year between 2005 and 2009 to the present rate of 20 to 25 project visits.[140] He identified "ever increasing costs of production in China" and "better access to the U.S. market" as important drivers behind this trend.[141]

North Carolina set up its China office in October 2010.[142] According to a North Carolina official, the office has "gone from very few Chinese project interests to weekly calls from Chinese government delegations."[143] The office receives inquiries of all varieties regarding greenfield investments, joint ventures, M&A deals, and EB-5 visas.[144] But the official said "a lot of the work in the last three years was just about getting established and getting word out that there is an office."[145] North Carolina's investment promotion is also occurring at the municipal level. In May 2013, Jill Swaine, the mayor of Huntersville, logged 25,000 miles on a ten-day trip through China, "learning about opportunities to get Chinese factories to move to [Huntersville]."[146]

Arkansas established its China office in 2002 and only has one representative. In contrast to her colleagues from South Carolina and Georgia, the Arkansas representative, Ms. Liu, has not seen a marked increase in requests from Chinese companies.[147] Instead, she has to conduct her own outreach to find prospective investors.[148] More so than its wealthier neighbors, Arkansas promotes investment in basic manufacturing sectors such as paper, steel, and food processing.[149] Ms. Liu stressed that the unionization rate in Arkansas, a right-to-work state, is less than 4 percent.[150]

At the opposite end of the spectrum from the southern states are Colorado and New Jersey, which do not have representative offices in China. Jeffrey King, Colorado's International Business Manager for the Asia Pacific, told Commission staff Colorado does not have a China office because it feels the returns on investment are "not quite there to merit it."[151] Instead, one of Colorado's strategies is to inquire periodically about prospective Chinese investors at the Chinese consulate in Chicago.[152] The consulate reciprocates by requesting information when a Chinese company wants to make an investment in the state.[153]

New Jersey, in turn, relies on an outside vendor with a China presence, focusing on Chinese companies in the higher-value industries of life sciences and IT that do not yet have a U.S. presence.[154] New Jersey officials also attend trade shows for specific industries. For example, at a recent biotechnology convention in San Diego, they hosted a Chinese delegation for an hour-long presentation on their state. An official at Choose New Jersey said that SelectUSA, a federal investment promotion program run by the DOC, has been quite helpful.[155] In one instance, New Jersey was unable to send its own staff to a trade show in China, but with SelectUSA's help hired someone locally to do promotional work on behalf of the state.[156]

Michigan and California are two of the prime recipients of Chinese investment. Both have undergone a process of closing their China offices due to budgetary constraints and reopening them in partnership with the private sector. Michigan's China office was open for five years in the early 2000s, then shut down temporarily, and reopened in September 2012 with support from the Michigan Economic Development Corporation (MEDC), a public-private partnership supported by multiple companies in the state of Michigan.[157] Michigan now appears to have a well-oiled operation in Shanghai. A Michigan official told Commission staff that Governor Snyder has traveled to China every year since taking office.[158] MEDC targets specific companies in China for recruitment and also advertises Michigan industries that are open for business, combining trade and investment promotion. Investment promotion staff in Michigan and in Shanghai share market information "seamlessly" in order "to make sure we capture opportunities."[159]

California closed its China office in the early 2000s when the state's Trade and Commerce Agency was shut down for budgetary reasons. The California Governor's Office of Business and Economic Development (GO-Biz) was created in 2012 to resuscitate the state government's business attraction and retention programs.[160] A bill authored that year by California Assembly Speaker John A. Perez (D-Los Angeles) allowed GO-Biz to create state trade and investment offices through public-private partnerships. It led to the reopening of the China office in April 2013, in the form of a public-private partnership with the Bay Area Council.[*] The Bay Area Council is raising approximately $1 million annually to operate the Shanghai-based office.[161] David Bolognesi, who formerly handled international investor relations for the state of California, commended this setup because "the state is represented abroad but eliminates any costs for the state."[162] In concert with the opening of the China office, California formed a partnership with China's MOFCOM to bolster economic ties and cooperation, the first of its kind between MOFCOM and a U.S. sub-national organization.[163]

However, Ms. Browning claims GO-Biz is not as generously funded as its counterparts in other states.[164] With only three staff conducting investment promotion, the office prefers to refer prospective investors to investment promotion officials at the municipal level.[165] San Francisco, Silicon Valley, and Los Angeles have their own representative offices in China.[166]

Several other states with a presence in China have traditionally emphasized trade over investment promotion. Mississippi and Pennsylvania each have a trade promotion office on the Mainland but conduct investment promotion activities out of Hong Kong and Taiwan.[167] Mr. Pruitt, the Missouri official, says his state's China office has historically focused more on trade than investment promotion, but is now broadening its mission.[168] The Missouri office values its partnerships with the St. Louis and Kansas City World Trade Centers,[†] which help to bring Chinese delegations (government officials, academics, business people) to the state and stimulate interest in priority industries such as agriculture, food processing, and general manufacturing.[169]

Iowa, a major exporter of farm goods to China, has maintained a contractor office with two full-time staff there for eight years. Although the state is looking to attract Chinese investors in industries like manufacturing, agriculture, and financial services, the most notable investment thus far is a $41 million downtown hotel in Muscatine, currently in the development phase.[170] Ann and Tom Meeker, owners of Muscatine Downtown Investors, planned the development and secured a 50-50 stake with Ruiling Liu, the president of YiBo Foundation Hebei International Trading Co., a trade company based in Hebei province, which has been Iowa's sister state for three decades. Supporting the project are state government tax incentives from Iowa's Reinvestment District program.[171]

Competition and Coordination among States

Increasingly, local governments in the United States are working together on China-focused investment promotion efforts. The SelectUSA program, established by executive order of President Barack Obama in June 2011 and housed within the DOC, has begun to step up its activities.[172] Under the program, several U.S. mayors toured China in the summer of 2012.[173] State officials told Commission staff they looked forward to SelectUSA's biennial Investment Summit, to be held March 2015 in Washington, DC.[174][‡] Some 75 Chinese companies, mostly real estate firms, had registered to attend by early February, the largest delegation of any country.[175]

Other investment promotion programs are regional in nature. In March 2014, for example, Dothan, a city of about 68,000 in southeast Alabama near the Georgia and Florida borders, joined with the Hong Kong-based economic development group SoZo to organize a U.S.-China manufacturing symposium. Four hundred Chinese and U.S. business and government leaders gathered at the Dothan Civic Center. At the event, the chief executive of an Alabama-based logistics firm told reporters:

---

* The Bay Area Council is a business-sponsored, public policy advocacy organization for the nine-county Bay Area. More than 275 of the largest employers in the region support the Bay Area Council and offer their CEO or top executive as a member. Bay Area Council, "About Us." *http://www.bayareacouncil.org/about-us/*.

† The World Trade Center St. Louis (WTC), established in 1993, has an operating license granted by the World Trade Centers Association (WTCA) in New York. It serves the entire Missouri and Southern Illinois markets, excluding the Kansas City region. It is a member of an extensive global association of over 300 World Trade Centers. World Trade Center St. Louis, "About the World Trade Center." *http://www.worldtradecenter-stl.com/aboutUs/indexAbout.asp*.

‡ For more information on the SelectUSA Investment Summit, visit *http://www.selectusasummit.com/*.

[The Chinese] can see the South and Alabama are willing to go the extra mile to help them. There's a certain friendliness that we have, there's a certain pro-business attitude that we have and there's definitely a pro-Chinese pro-foreign investment attitude that we have....You see companies, governmental units and economic development units all here together, all working well together and willing to do whatever is necessary so [Chinese] companies will not be alone when they get here.[176]

However, states also compete with one another to attract investment. Ms. Liu, the Arkansas state official, affirmed Chinese companies "shop around" when they consider where to invest, and the states that offer the best conditions often win.[177] She said the Arkansas office always provides some form of incentives to prospective Chinese investors, as do most other states.[178] The mayor of Dallas, Texas, stated during a promotional trip to China in 2012:

We are very aggressive with taxes and incentives. As businesses move in, we would offer them tax abatements for periods of time if they are able to create jobs. And for individual investors we have a program called Dallas Regional Center where individuals can invest in Dallas and get some benefits from green card status as well. We also have two free-trade zones, one in the Dallas airport and one in the City of Dallas.[179]

If a local government commits a Chinese company to a project, additional work is required to make it a success. Mr. Gillenwater said that in Maryland, managers from Taiwan are more in tune with U.S. business practices than mainland Chinese investors.[180] Chinese companies also hire U.S. consultants less often than investors from Western developed countries, preferring instead to lean on local officials.[181] A California official noted that while European and Japanese investors have a global profile, Chinese investors purchase assets in the United States foremost as an outlet for their domestic business. Lacking experience, they expect the local government to work on their behalf.[182] Mr. Pruitt, the Missouri official, told the Commission: "I think there's a disconnect between what [Chinese investors] think a local official can do and what a local official can actually do when it comes to permits and incentives."[183]

Academic and Research Cooperation

An alternative method of attracting Chinese investors to the United States is through academic and research institutions. The benefit of this approach is it builds on the U.S. competitive advantage in higher education, and helps integrate Chinese nationals into the fabric of U.S. society. Mr. Bolognesi cited the example of the semiconductor company Marvel Technology Group Ltd.,* which was started in 1995 by a Chinese graduate of University of California (UC) Berkeley. Several other Chinese graduate students trained in California have gone on to start IT companies there.[184]

R&D partnerships with Chinese universities can serve as source of funding to U.S. schools. Recently, the Scripps Institute of Oceanography at UC San Diego (UCSD) signed an agreement with Ningbo University. It includes $50 to $100 million of Chinese funding for a Scripps/UCSD research center for development of renewable marine resources and technologies at Ningbo University, and the formation of a $25 million marine innovation and technology fund for commercialization in China of Scripps/UCSD discoveries.[185]

A different type of program is being carried out at the University of Maryland (UM) International Incubator, a partnership between the state of Maryland and the UM School of Engineering. Its objective is to help foreign companies set up small business development and R&D operations in the United States.[186] Dr. Kai Duh, who helps bring Chinese companies to the incubator, told Commission staff he was recruited seven years ago by UM to help launch the program. From the outset, he worked closely with the Maryland Department of Business and Economic Development, which actively supports the incubator as a means of attracting foreign businesses to the state.[187]

According to Dr. Duh, during the last six years or so of operation, the incubator has recruited about 24 companies from China (two out of every three companies in the incubator are Chinese).[188] UM has signed a formal agreement with China's Ministry of Science and Technology, which advertises UM to Chinese companies as a good place to

---

* Founded in 1995, Marvell Technology Group Ltd. has operations worldwide and more than 7,000 employees. Marvell's U.S. operating subsidiary is based in Santa Clara, California, and Marvell has international design centers located in China, Europe, Hong Kong, India, Israel, Japan, Malaysia, Singapore, Taiwan, and the United States. A leading fabless semiconductor company, Marvell ships over one billion chips a year. "About Marvell Technology Group Ltd." *http://www.marvell.com/company/.*

improve entrepreneurship and innovation. The Chinese companies selected are mostly small- and medium-sized enterprises, typically with 50 to 100 people in the whole company.[189] One of the larger players is Glodon, a Beijing-based company that markets Architecture, Engineering, and Construction/Information Technology (AEC/IT) goods and services. It is listed on the Shenzhen Stock Exchange and has some 3,000 staff worldwide.* Glodon has four full-time staff at the Maryland incubator.[190]

Dr. Duh said most Chinese companies at the incubator send one or two executives from headquarters and hire a couple of student interns from campus. After a couple of years, some of the interns who graduate are hired to be full-time employees.[191] Chinese company staff collaborate with UM faculty on new products, services, and marketing strategies; take UM courses on entrepreneurship; and receive advice on U.S. laws regarding product liability, employment, and other matters.[192]

Implications for the United States

China's investment in the United States is maturing in terms of both aggregate capital flows and local deal making. As the Chinese government takes steps to relax restrictions on outbound investment, more Chinese companies are likely to arrive on U.S. shores, even as those already present reinvest their profits in business expansion. Concurrently, wealthy Chinese individuals are flooding into the U.S. property market in search of lucrative assets and the opportunity to live and work outside China.

These trends have important implications for U.S. policy that merit further consideration:

- *Regulation of the EB-5 visa program could be improved.* In theory, EB-5 investors can stimulate the U.S. economy by generating employment. However, the program was not designed to accommodate such a high number of applicants from one country. There is currently no sign of abatement in Chinese applicants; indeed, China's ongoing anticorruption campaign could accelerate the offshoring of wealth by the country's elite. At the same time, a number of poorly executed and fraudulent EB-5 projects have surfaced. Given that USCIS is tasked primarily with customs and immigration matters, it is questionable whether this federal agency has the capability to properly oversee the economic dimension of the EB-5 application process at the local level—in particular, the quality of TEA certificates issued to Chinese investors. Stemming the flow of Chinese applicants could require modifying the quota system and/or improving vetting of EB-5 projects.

- *Clarifying the role of federal programs and national initiatives.* Foreign investment into the United States can deliver aggregate benefits to the U.S. economy. More could be done, however, to assist local governments in assessing the risks and opportunities associated with Chinese investment. CASIC and SelectUSA are examples of programs that can help local officials attract business from China. In parallel, coordination with relevant U.S. authorities could help U.S. states evaluate the implications of Chinese investments in critical infrastructure and technologies, especially when these are undertaken by state-owned and state-invested enterprises. Although investments into the United States that do not involve "controlling" acquisitions of U.S. entities are not required to be reviewed by the Committee on Foreign Investment in the United States, there are risks worth considering.†

- *If done right, local research incubators can make a positive impact.* The research incubator at College Park, Maryland, serves as a positive example of how Chinese companies can be integrated into innovative sectors of the U.S. economy. China is now an important stakeholder in global innovation. Bilateral R&D cooperation can deliver economic as well as societal benefits in fields such as

---

* Glodon Software Company Limited, founded in 1998, listed on the Shenzhen Small and Medium Enterprise (SME) Board (stock name: GLD, stock code: 002410) in May 2010, making it the first listed company in China's AEC/IT industry. Its clients include constructors, owners, design institutes, intermediary agencies, material vendors, property companies, universities, and governments. In 2008, the company began to pursue overseas business opportunities. In addition to a U.S. subsidiary company, it has established Singapore and Hong Kong subsidiaries to enter the Southeast Asian market. Glodon, "Company Profile." *http://en.glodon.com/aboutus/glodon/intro.*

† For additional analysis on the national security risks pertaining to Chinese investment, see U.S.-China Economic and Security Review Commission, *2013 Annual Report to Congress*, November 2013, Chapter 1.2. The report can be accessed at *http://www.uscc.gov.*

pharmaceuticals, biotechnology, and clean energy. China's small and medium-sized private enterprises value the skilled workers and know-how offered by the United States. Such companies are distinct from the large Chinese conglomerates that enjoy privileged access to state-owned bank loans and prefer direct acquisitions of U.S. companies. An important prerequisite for stronger R&D cooperation, however, is strong regulatory oversight, given the repeated incidences of intellectual property theft and forced technology transfer involving Chinese companies.

- *Adherence to U.S. labor and environmental laws is a priority issue.* As real wages rise in China and the RMB appreciates against the dollar, the United States is becoming an attractive destination for some Chinese manufacturers, particularly those looking to sell into the United States and to profit from the recent decline in U.S. energy costs. Because labor and environmental laws are not as rigorous and well-enforced in China as in the United States, it is important to ensure Chinese investors abide by the relevant U.S. laws and norms, and that this occurs uniformly across all U.S. states.

- *Foreign investment from China is not sufficient to rebalance the bilateral economic relationship.* The United States recorded another record trade deficit with China in 2014, and China has not meaningfully reduced its purchases of U.S. treasury bills. In sectors such as automotive manufacturing, agriculture, and services, China has not afforded a reciprocal level of market access to U.S. investors.

Endnotes

[1] Daniel Rosen and Thilo Hanemann, *New Realities in the U.S.-China Investment Relationship* (Rhodium Group, April 29, 2014). *http://rhg.com/notes/newrealities-in-the-us-china-investment-relationship.*

[2] Fion Li and Kyoungwha Kim, "China's Reserves Retreat from $4 Trillion Mark as Outflows Seen," Bloomberg, October 16, 2014. *http://www.bloomberg.com/news/articles/2014-10-16/china-s-reserves-retreat-from-4-trillion-mark-as-outflows-seen.*

[3] Data from China State Administration of Foreign Exchange, via CEIC.

[4] Data from World Bank. *http://data.worldbank.org/indicator/FI.RES.TOTL.CD.*

[5] China State Administration of Foreign Exchange, via CEIC.

[6] Dina Gusovsky, "Why Chinese Money Is Flooding American Markets," CNBC, September 17, 2014. *http://www.cnbc.com/id/102001876#.*

[7] Dexter Roberts, "China Buys Foreign Companies at a Record Pace," Bloomberg, October 30, 2014. *http://www.businessweek.com/articles/2014-10-30/asset-hungry-chinese-firms-to-spend-120-billion-in-overseas-purchases-this-year.*

[8] China's International Investment Position (IIP) data from the China State Administration of Foreign Exchange, via CEIC.

[9] Wendy Pan, Ning Zhang, and Aaron Xin, "New MOFCOM Rules to Further Facilitate China Outbound Investments," O'Melveny & Myers LLP, September 22, 2014. *http://www.omm.com/new-mofcom-rules-to-further-facilitate-china-outbound-investments/.*

[10] Wendy Pan, Ning Zhang, and Aaron Xin, "New MOFCOM Rules to Further Facilitate China Outbound Investments," O'Melveny & Myers LLP, September 22, 2014. *http://www.omm.com/new-mofcom-rules-to-further-facilitate-china-outbound-investments/.*

[11] Rhodium Group, *Chinese FDI in the United States: Q3 2014 Update* (October 2014). *http://rhg.com/notes/chinese-fdi-in-the-united-states-q3-2014-update.*

[12] Hogan Lovells, "China Moves to Further Relax Approval Requirements on Outbound Investments by Chinese Investors: A Step in the Right Direction," February 2015. *http://www.hoganlovells.com/files/Publication/f2f8736c-c04e-4e48-9aff-de1c1fba1222/Presentation/PublicationAttachment/a95af001-7bb6-46df-bf75-f1392467dbf4/HKGLIB01-1099746-v3-Novell_Hong_Kong_Limited_-_SP_approving_change_of_company_name.pdf;* Wendy Pan, Ning Zhang, and Aaron Xin, "New MOFCOM Rules to Further Facilitate China Outbound Investments," O'Melveny & Myers LLP, September 22, 2014. *http://www.omm.com/new-mofcom-rules-to-further-facilitate-china-outbound-investments/.*

[13] Hogan Lovells, "China Moves to Further Relax Approval Requirements on Outbound Investments by Chinese Investors: A Step in the Right Direction," February 2015. *http://www.hoganlovells.com/files/Publication/f2f8736c-c04e-4e48-9aff-de1c1fba1222/Presentation/PublicationAttachment/a95af001-7bb6-46df-bf75-f1392467dbf4/HKGLIB01-1099746-v3-Novell_Hong_Kong_Limited_-_SP_approving_change_of_company_name.pdf;* Wendy Pan, Ning Zhang, and Aaron Xin, "New MOFCOM Rules to Further Facilitate China Outbound Investments," O'Melveny & Myers LLP, September 22, 2014. *http://www.omm.com/new-mofcom-rules-to-further-facilitate-china-outbound-investments/.*

[14] Hogan Lovells, "China Moves to Further Relax Approval Requirements on Outbound Investments by Chinese Investors: A Step in the Right Direction," February 2015. *http://www.hoganlovells.com/files/Publication/f2f8736c-c04e-4e48-9aff-de1c1fba1222/Presentation/PublicationAttachment/a95af001-7bb6-46df-bf75-f1392467dbf4/HKGLIB01-1099746-v3-Novell_Hong_Kong_Limited_-_SP_approving_change_of_company_name.pdf.*

[15] Rhodium Group, *Chinese FDI in the United States: Q3 2014 Update* (October 2014). *http://rhg.com/notes/chinese-fdi-in-the-united-states-q3-2014-update.*

[16] Data from the U.S Bureau of Economic Analysis, via CEIC.

[17] Data from the U.S Bureau of Economic Analysis, via CEIC.

[18] Data from the Heritage Foundation and China State Administration of Foreign Exchange, via CEIC.

[19] Daniel Rosen and Thilo Hanemann, *New Realities in the U.S.-China Investment Relationship* (Rhodium Group, April 29, 2014). *http://rhg.com/notes/newrealities-in-the-us-china-investment-relationship.*

[20] International Monetary Fund, *World Economic Outlook*, January 20, 2015. *http://www.imf.org/external/pubs/ft/weo/2015/update/01/pdf/0115.pdf;* Peter Hooper, Michael Spencer, and Torsten Slok, *Global Economic Perspectives: Notes from China* (Deutsche Bank, January 16, 2015), p. 2.

[21] Angela Monaghan, "U.S. Federal Reserve to End Quantitative Easing Programme," *Guardian*, October 29, 2014. *http://www.theguardian.com/business/2014/oct/29/us-federal-reserve-end-quantitative-easing-programme.*

[22] Exchange rate data from OANDA. *http://www.oanda.com/;* Andrew Burns et al., "Unconventional Monetary Policy Normalisation and Emerging-Market Capital Flows," VOX, January 21, 2014. *http://www.voxeu.org/article/tapering-and-emerging-market-capital-flows.*

[23] Rhodium Group, *Chinese FDI in the United States: Q4 2014 and Full Year Update* (January 2015). *http://rhg.com/notes/chinese-fdi-in-the-united-states-q4-and-full-year-2014-update.*

[24] Rhodium Group, *Chinese FDI in the United States: Q4 2014 and Full Year Update* (January 2015). *http://rhg.com/notes/chinese-fdi-in-the-united-states-q4-and-full-year-2014-update.*

[25] Rhodium Group, *Chinese FDI in the United States: Q4 2014 and Full Year Update* (January 2015). *http://rhg.com/notes/chinese-fdi-in-the-united-states-q4-and-full-year-2014-update.*

[26] State of California, *California Opens Trade and Investment Office in China*, April 11, 2013. *http://gov.ca.gov/news.php?id=17994.*

[27] Cushman & Wakefield, *China's Outbound Boom: The Rise of Chinese Investment in Global Real Estate* (October 2014), p. 6. *http://www.cushmanwakefield.com/~/media/global-reports/CHINASOUTBOUNDBOOM_EN2410.pdf.*

[28] Paul J. Davies, "Chinese Group Loads up with Debt to Pay for U.S. Foodmaker," *Financial Times*, June 11, 2013. *http://www.ft.com/intl/cms/s/0/aa8a2628-cf55-11e2-be7b-00144feab7de.html#axzz3QbzlJERM;* Sally Bakewell, "Goldwind Signs $5.5

Billion China Development Bank Wind Pact," *Bloomberg*, January 31, 2012. *http://www.bloomberg.com/news/2012-01-31/goldwind-signs-5-5-billion-china-development-bank-pact-for-wind.html.*

29 Rhodium Group, *Chinese FDI in the United States: Q3 2014 Update* (October 2014). *http://rhg.com/notes/chinese-fdi-in-the-united-states-q3-2014-update.*

30 FTI Consulting, *Chinese Deals under the Microscope: Looking at the Evolving CFIUS Process* (2014). *www.fticonsulting.com.*

31 FTI Consulting, *Chinese Deals under the Microscope: Looking at the Evolving CFIUS Process* (2014). *www.fticonsulting.com.*

32 FTI Consulting, *Chinese Deals under the Microscope: Looking at the Evolving CFIUS Process* (2014). *www.fticonsulting.com.*

33 FTI Consulting, *Chinese Deals under the Microscope: Looking at the Evolving CFIUS Process* (2014). *www.fticonsulting.com.*

34 Eliot Brown and Lingling Wei, "New York Skyscraper Is Latest Property Deal for Chinese," *Wall Street Journal*, December 8, 2014. *http://www.wsj.com/articles/new-york-skyscraper-is-latest-property-deal-for-chinese-1418091603.*

35 Cushman & Wakefield, telephone interview with Commission staff, November 4, 2014.

36 Zachary R. Mider, "China's Wanda to Buy AMC Cinema Chain for $2.6 Billion," *Bloomberg*, May 21, 2012. *http://www.bloomberg.com/news/2012-05-21/china-s-wanda-group-to-buy-amc-cinema-chain-for-2-6-billion.html*; Cushman & Wakefield, telephone interview with Commission staff, November 4, 2014.

37 Heather Perlberg, "Hilton to Sell NYC's Waldorf Astoria to Chinese Insurer for $1.95 Billion," *Bloomberg*, October 6, 2014. *http://www.bloomberg.com/news/print/2014-10-06/hilton-to-sell-nyc-s-waldorf-astoria-or-1-95-billion.html.*

38 Cushman & Wakefield, *China's Outbound Boom: The Rise of Chinese Investment in Global Real Estate* (October 2014), p. 6. *http://www.cushmanwakefield.com/~/media/global-reports/CHINASOUTBOUNDBOOM_EN2410.pdf.*

39 Cushman & Wakefield, telephone interview with Commission staff, November 4, 2014.

40 Cushman & Wakefield, telephone interview with Commission staff, November 4, 2014.

41 David Briel (Executive Director, Pennsylvania Center for Direct Investment), interview with Commission staff, November 5, 2014.

42 Bradley Gillenwater (Regional Manager for Asia, Maryland Department of Business and Economic Development), interview with Commission staff, August 18, 2014; Dennis Pruitt (Vice President of International Business Recruitment, Missouri Partnership), interview with Commission staff, August 18, 2014.

43 Bradley Gillenwater (Regional Manager for Asia, Maryland Department of Business and Economic Development), interview with Commission staff, February 3, 2015.

44 Official at North Carolina State Economic Development Representative, telephone interview with Commission staff, August 18, 2014.

45 Cushman & Wakefield, telephone interview with Commission staff, November 4, 2014.

46 Karen Wise, "Why Are Chinese Millionaires Buying Mansions in an L.A. Suburb?" *Businessweek*, October 15, 2014. *http://www.businessweek.com/articles/2014-10-15/chinese-home-buying-binge-transforms-california-suburb-arcadia.*

47 Jack Detsch, "Chinese Investors Fuel California Housing Bubble," *Diplomat* (Tokyo), October 30, 2014. *http://thediplomat.com/2014/08/chinese-investors-fuel-california-housing-bubble/?allpages=yes&print=yes.*

48 Lawrence Yun, Jed Smith, and Gay Cororaton, *2014 Profile of International Home Buying Activity* (National Association of Realtors, June 2014).

49 Jack Detsch, "Chinese Investors Fuel California Housing Bubble," *Diplomat* (Tokyo), October 30, 2014. *http://thediplomat.com/2014/08/chinese-investors-fuel-california-housing-bubble/?allpages=yes&print=yes.*

50 Jack Detsch, "Chinese Investors Fuel California Housing Bubble," *Diplomat* (Tokyo), October 30, 2014. *http://thediplomat.com/2014/08/chinese-investors-fuel-california-housing-bubble/?allpages=yes&print=yes.*

51 Cushman & Wakefield, telephone interview with Commission staff, November 4, 2014.

52 Marina Walker Guevara et al., *Leaked Records Reveal Offshore Holdings of China's Elite* (The International Consortium of Investigative Journalists, January 21, 2014). *http://www.icij.org/offshore/leaked-records-reveal-offshore-holdings-chinas-elite.*

53 Marina Walker Guevara et al., *Leaked Records Reveal Offshore Holdings of China's Elite* (The International Consortium of Investigative Journalists, January 21, 2014). *http://www.icij.org/offshore/leaked-records-reveal-offshore-holdings-chinas-elite.*

54 Karen Weise, "Why Are Chinese Millionaires Buying Mansion in an L.A. Suburb?" *Businessweek*, October 15, 2014. *http://www.businessweek.com/articles/2014-10-15/chinese-home-buying-binge-transforms-california-suburb-arcadia.*

55 "China's Capital Account – An Open and Shut Case," *Wall Street Journal*, February 25, 2014. *http://blogs.wsj.com/chinarealtime/2014/02/25/chinas-capital-account-an-open-and-shut-case/.*

56 Karen Weise, "Why Are Chinese Millionaires Buying Mansion in an L.A. Suburb?" *Businessweek*, October 15, 2014. *http://www.businessweek.com/articles/2014-10-15/chinese-home-buying-binge-transforms-california-suburb-arcadia.*

57 James Kynge, "Fake China Export Invoices Surge Again – Survey," *Financial Times*, October 3, 2014. *http://blogs.ft.com/beyond-brics/2014/10/03/fake-china-export-invoices-surge-again-survey/.*

58 Dezan Shira and Associates, "China to Lower Incorporation Requirements," *Caijing* (English edition), February 26, 2014. *http://english.caijing.com.cn/2014-02-26/113960317.html.*

59 Ali Jahangiri, "Chinese EB-5 Visa Retrogression: Good for Program Diversity," *Huffington Post*, November 25, 2014. *http://www.huffingtonpost.com/ali-jahangiri/chinese-eb5-visa-retrogre_b_5884602.html*; Mona Shah and Yi Song, "EB-5 Retrogression for China in Mid-2014 – Not Really a Reason to Be Alarmed?" LexisNexis, January 22, 2014. *http://www.lexisnexis.com/legalnewsroom/banking/b/venture-capital/archive/2014/01/22/eb-5-retrogression-for-china-in-mid-2014-not-really-a-reason-to-be-alarmed.aspx.*

60 Rhodium Group, *Chinese FDI in the United States: Q1 2014 Update* (May 2014). *http://rhg.com/notes/chinese-fdi-in-the-united-states-q3-2014-update.*

61 Miriam Jordan, "Investor Visas Soaked up by Chinese," *Wall Street Journal*, August 27, 2014. *http://www.wsj.com/articles/investor-visas-soaked-up-by-chinese-1409095982.*

62 Miriam Jordan, "Investor Visas Soaked up by Chinese," *Wall Street Journal*, August 27, 2014. *http://www.wsj.com/articles/investor-visas-soaked-up-by-chinese-1409095982.*

63 Lindsay Liu (Chief Representative, The China Office of Arkansas Economic Development Commission), e-mail to Commission staff, November 2, 2014.

64 Seth Jacobs (Managing Director for Investment, State of Georgia in China), e-mail to Commission staff, November 10, 2014.

65 John Ling (Managing Director for China, South Carolina Department of Commerce), e-mail to Commission staff, November 3, 2014.

66 David Briel (Executive Director, Center for Direct Investment, State of Pennsylvania), e-mail to Commission staff, November 5, 2014.

67 Wei Gu, "Chinese-Buffett Deal Food for Thought for Seekers of U.S. Visas," *Wall Street Journal*, January 29, 2015. *http://www.wsj.com/articles/chinese-buffett-deal-food-for-thought-for-seekers-of-u-s-visas-1422518511?mod=WSJ_hp_EditorsPicks.*

68 Official at Michigan Economic Development Corporation, interview with Commission staff, August 27, 2014.

69 Peter Elkind and Marty Jones, "The Dark Disturbing World of the Visa-for-Sale Program," *Fortune*, July 24, 2014. *http://fortune.com/2014/07/24/immigration-eb-5-visa-for-sale/.*

70 Abigail L. Browning (International Policy, Planning and Partnership International Affairs and Business Development, California Governor's Office of Business and Economic Development), interview with Commission staff, February 3, 2015.

71 Data from Stats America and U.S. Citizenship and Immigration Services.

72 U.S. Citizenship and Immigration Services, *Memorandum: Adjudication of EB-5 Regional Center Proposals and Affiliated Form I-526 and Form I-829 Petitions*, December 2009, p. 3. *http://www.uscis.gov/sites/default/files/USCIS/Laws/Memoranda/Static%20Files%20Memoranda/Adjudicating%20of%20EB-5_121109.pdf.*

73 U.S. Citizenship and Immigration Services, *Immigrant Investor Regional Centers. http://www.uscis.gov/working-united-states/permanent-workers/employment-based-immigration-fifth-preference-eb-5/immigrant-investor-regional-centers.*

74 Peter Elkind and Marty Jones, "The Dark Disturbing World of the Visa-for-Sale Program," *Fortune*, July 24, 2014. *http://fortune.com/2014/07/24/immigration-eb-5-visa-for-sale/.*

75 Peter Elkind and Marty Jones, "The Dark Disturbing World of the Visa-for-Sale Program," *Fortune*, July 24, 2014. *http://fortune.com/2014/07/24/immigration-eb-5-visa-for-sale/.*

76 Abigail L. Browning (International Policy, Planning and Partnership International Affairs and Business Development, California Governor's Office of Business and Economic Development), interview with Commission staff, February 3, 2015.

77 Abigail L. Browning (International Policy, Planning and Partnership International Affairs and Business Development, California Governor's Office of Business and Economic Development), interview with Commission staff, February 3, 2015.

78 Washington State Employment Security Department, *EB-5 Investor Targeted Employment Areas. https://fortress.wa.gov/esd/employmentdata/reports-publications/regional-reports/eb-5-investor-targeted-employment-areas.*

79 Abigail L. Browning (International Policy, Planning and Partnership International Affairs and Business Development, California Governor's Office of Business and Economic Development), interview with Commission staff, February 3, 2015.

80 Abigail L. Browning (International Policy, Planning and Partnership International Affairs and Business Development, California Governor's Office of Business and Economic Development), interview with Commission staff, February 3, 2015.

81 Abigail L. Browning (International Policy, Planning and Partnership International Affairs and Business Development, California Governor's Office of Business and Economic Development), interview with Commission staff, February 3, 2015.

82 Abigail L. Browning (International Policy, Planning and Partnership International Affairs and Business Development, California Governor's Office of Business and Economic Development), interview with Commission staff, February 3, 2015.

83 Peter Elkind and Marty Jones, "The Dark Disturbing World of the Visa-for-Sale Program," *Fortune*, July 24, 2014. *http://fortune.com/2014/07/24/immigration-eb-5-visa-for-sale/.*

84 Abigail L. Browning (International Policy, Planning and Partnership International Affairs and Business Development, California Governor's Office of Business and Economic Development), interview with Commission staff, February 3, 2015.

85 Abigail L. Browning (International Policy, Planning and Partnership International Affairs and Business Development, California Governor's Office of Business and Economic Development), interview with Commission staff, February 3, 2015.

86 Abigail L. Browning (International Policy, Planning and Partnership International Affairs and Business Development, California Governor's Office of Business and Economic Development), interview with Commission staff, February 3, 2015.

87 Abigail L. Browning (International Policy, Planning and Partnership International Affairs and Business Development, California Governor's Office of Business and Economic Development), interview with Commission staff, February 3, 2015.

88 Abigail L. Browning (International Policy, Planning and Partnership International Affairs and Business Development, California Governor's Office of Business and Economic Development), interview with Commission staff, February 3, 2015.

89 Bradley Gillenwater (Regional Manager for Asia, Maryland Department of Business and Economic Development), interview with Commission staff, February 3, 2015.

90 U.S. Attorney's Office – Northern District of Illinois, "Chicago Man Allegedly Exploited U.S. Visa Program to Defraud Chinese Investors of $160 Million in Purported O'Hare Complex," Justice Department FBI Press Releases, August 27, 2014, via Factiva; Peter Elkind and Marty Jones, "The Dark Disturbing World of the Visa-for-Sale Program," *Fortune*, July 24, 2014. *http://fortune.com/2014/07/24/immigration-eb-5-visa-for-sale/.*

91 Sean Sullivan, "FBI Investigating South Dakota EB-5 Program, A Potential Blow to Senate GOP," *Washington Post*, October 22, 2014, via Factiva.

92 Peter Elkind and Marty Jones, "The Dark Disturbing World of the Visa-for-Sale Program," *Fortune*, July 24, 2014. *http://fortune.com/2014/07/24/immigration-eb-5-visa-for-sale/*; NPR: Weekend All Things Considered, "Investing in Citizenship: For the Rich, a Road to the U.S.," National Public Radio, January 26, 2013, via Factiva.

93 *Converting Quarterly*, "China's Uniscite to Build New SC BOPP-Film Plant," February 1, 2012. *http://www.convertingquarterly.com/industry-news/articles/id/3849/chinas-uniscite-to-build-new-sc-bopp-film-plant.aspx*; John Ling (Managing Director for China, South Carolina Department of Commerce), e-mail to Commission staff, November 3, 2014.

94 Massoud Hayoun, "China's Louisiana Purchase: Who's Building a Methanol Plant on the Bayou?" *Al Jazeera* (U.S. edition), January 26, 2015. *http://america.aljazeera.com/articles/2015/1/26/chinas-louisiana-jindal-methanol-plant-environment-racism.html.*

95 Massoud Hayoun, "China's Louisiana Purchase: Who's Building a Methanol Plant on the Bayou?" *Al Jazeera* (U.S. edition), January 26, 2015. *http://america.aljazeera.com/articles/2015/1/26/chinas-louisiana-jindal-methanol-plant-environment-racism.html.*

96 David Briel (Executive Director, Center for Direct Investment, State of Pennsylvania), e-mail to Commission staff, November 5, 2014.

97 John Ling (Managing Director for China, South Carolina Department of Commerce), e-mail to Commission staff, November 3, 2014.

98 Dinny McMahon, "Spotted Again in America: Textile Jobs," *Wall Street Journal*, December 22, 2013, via Factiva.

99 Dinny McMahon, "Spotted Again in America: Textile Jobs," *Wall Street Journal*, December 22, 2013, via Factiva.

100 U.S.-China Economic and Security Review Commission, *Hearing on China's Agriculture Policy and U.S. Access to China's Market*, testimony of Mark Lange, April 25, 2013; "India's Cotton Exports Hit as China Shifts Policy," Reuters, April 17, 2014. *http://in.reuters.com/article/2014/04/17/india-cotton-exports-idINL4N0MP2MK20140417*; and Official at North Carolina State Economic Development Representative, telephone interview with Commission staff, August 18, 2014.

101 Dennis Pruitt (Vice President of International Business Recruitment, Missouri Partnership), interview with Commission staff, February 3, 2015.

102 Dennis Pruitt (Vice President of International Business Recruitment, Missouri Partnership), interview with Commission staff, February 3, 2015.

103 *Inside U.S. Trade*, "DOC Levels High Final Duties on Chinese and Taiwanese Solar Products," December 19, 2014. *http://chinatradeextra.com/Inside-US-Trade/Inside-U.S.-Trade-12/19/2014/doc-levels-high-final-duties-on-chinese-and-taiwanese-solar-products/menu-id-710.html.*

104 Official at North Carolina State Economic Development Representative, telephone interview with Commission staff, August 18, 2014.

105 Official at North Carolina State Economic Development Representative, telephone interview with Commission staff, August 18, 2014.

106 North Carolina Department of Agriculture and Consumer Services, *Press Release: China Tobacco International Opens Company in N.C.*, June 27, 2013. *http://www.ncagr.gov/paffairs/release/2013/6-13-China-Tobacco-to-open-NC-office.htm.*

107 Official at North Carolina State Economic Development Representative, telephone interview with Commission staff, August 18, 2014.

108 North Carolina Department of Agriculture and Consumer Services, *Press Release: China Tobacco International Opens Company in N.C.*, June 27, 2013. *http://www.ncagr.gov/paffairs/release/2013/6-13-China-Tobacco-to-open-NC-office.htm.*

109 North Carolina Department of Agriculture and Consumer Services, *Press Release: China Tobacco International Opens Company in N.C.*, June 27, 2013. *http://www.ncagr.gov/paffairs/release/2013/6-13-China-Tobacco-to-open-NC-office.htm.*

110 World Health Organization, *Report on the Global Tobacco Epidemic* (2013), p. 276.

111 National Park Service (Mississippi), *Asian Carp Overview*. *http://www.nps.gov/miss/naturescience/ascarpover.htm.*

112 Dennis Pruitt (Vice President of International Business Recruitment, Missouri Partnership), interview with Commission staff, February 3, 2015.

113 Annie Lowrey and Keith Bradsher, "U.S. Gains in a Spat with China over Tariffs," *New York Times*, May 23, 2014. *http://www.nytimes.com/2014/05/24/business/wto-ruling-on-chinese-tariffs-on-us-cars.html?_r=0.*

114 U.S. Bureau of Economic Analysis, *U.S. International Trade in Goods and Services*, December 2014, p. 23. *http://www.bea.gov/newsreleases/international/trade/2015/pdf/trad1214.pdf.*

115 Regina Abrami et al., *Wanxiang Group: A Chinese Company's Global Strategy*, HBS Case Collection (Cambridge, MA: Harvard Business School, February 2008).

116 Fisker Automotive, "Our History." *http://thenewfisker.com/past/.*

117 Gordon G. Chang, "China's Wanxiang Challenges Tesla for Dominance of Global Electrics Market," *Forbes*, June 29, 2014. *http://www.forbes.com/sites/gordonchang/2014/06/29/chinas-wanxiang-challenges-tesla-for-dominance-of-global-electrics-market/.*

118 Dennis Pruitt (Vice President of International Business Recruitment, Missouri Partnership), interview with Commission staff, February 3, 2015.

119 Office of Missouri Governor Jay Nixon, *Major Auto Supplier Plans to Build New Manufacturing Facility in Riverside, Expected to Create 263 Jobs, Gov. Nixon Announces*, April 26, 2013. *http://governor.mo.gov/news/archive/major-auto-supplier-plans-build-new-manufacturing-facility-riverside-expected-create.*

120 Official at Michigan Economic Development Corporation, interview with Commission staff, August 27, 2014.

121 Official at Michigan Economic Development Corporation, interview with Commission staff, August 27, 2014.

122 Kathryn Lynch-Morin, "New Chapter Begins Today for Saginaw's Nexteer after Purchase by Chinese Auto-Parts Maker Announced," *Saginaw News*, July 8, 2010. *http://www.mlive.com/business/mid-michigan/index.ssf/2010/07/buena_vista_townships_nexteer.html.*

123 Kathryn Lynch-Morin, "Nexteer's Parent Acquired: Company Says Move Positions It for Growth," MLive Media Group, April 12, 2011. *http://www.mlive.com/business/mid-michigan/index.ssf/2011/04/nexteers_parent_acquired_compa.html.*

124 Official at Michigan Economic Development Corporation, interview with Commission staff, August 27, 2014.

125 Dexter Roberts, "China Buys Foreign Companies at a Record Pace," Bloomberg, October 30, 2014. *http://www.businessweek.com/articles/2014-10-30/asset-hungry-chinese-firms-to-spend-120-billion-in-overseas-purchases-this-year.*

126 Brenda Goh, "China Trainmakers CSR, CNR in Talks to Merge: State Media," Reuters, October 28, 2014. *http://www.reuters.com/article/2014/10/28/us-china-cnr-csr-corp-m-a-idUSKBN0IH01J20141028?type=companyNews.*

127 Scott Cohn, "Bay Bridge Project: Lost Opportunity for US Jobs?" CNBC, June 1, 2012. *http://www.cnbc.com/id/47631526#.*

128 Bradley Gillenwater (Regional Manager for Asia, Maryland Department of Business and Economic Development), interview with Commission staff, February 3, 2015.

129 Bradley Gillenwater (Regional Manager for Asia, Maryland Department of Business and Economic Development), interview with Commission staff, February 3, 2015.

130 Sam Sanders, "Construction Begins on California's $68 Billion High-Speed Rail Line," National Public Radio, January 6, 2015. *http://www.npr.org/blogs/thetwo-way/2015/01/06/375500902/construction-begins-on-californias-68-billion-high-speed-rail-line.*

131 *San Jose Mercury News*, "Governor Jerry Brown Goes to China in Seeking Investment in California," April 7, 2013. *http://www.mercurynews.com/ci_22975110/governor-jerry-brown-goes-china-seeking-investment-california.*

132 Ralph Vartabedian, "Bullet Train Just a Blur in California Governor's Race," *Los Angeles Times*, October 28, 2014. *http://www.latimes.com/local/politics/la-me-campaign-train-20141028-story.html#page=1.*

133 BIO International Convention, "JOINN Laboratories Inc." *https://mybio.org/exhibitor/member/81426.*

134 State of California, *California Opens Trade and Investment Office in China*, April 11, 2013. *http://gov.ca.gov/news.php?id=17994.*

135 Bradley Gillenwater (Regional Manager for Asia, Maryland Department of Business and Economic Development), interview with Commission staff, February 3, 2015.

136 Bradley Gillenwater (Regional Manager for Asia, Maryland Department of Business and Economic Development), interview with Commission staff, August 18, 2014.

137 Seth Jacobs (Managing Director for Investment, State of Georgia in China), e-mail to Commission staff, November 10, 2014.

138 John Ling (Managing Director for China, South Carolina Department of Commerce), e-mail to Commission staff, November 3, 2014.

139 John Ling (Managing Director for China, South Carolina Department of Commerce), e-mail to Commission staff, November 3, 2014.

140 John Ling (Managing Director for China, South Carolina Department of Commerce), e-mail to Commission staff, November 3, 2014.

141 John Ling (Managing Director for China, South Carolina Department of Commerce), e-mail to Commission staff, November 3, 2014.

142 North Carolina Biotechnology Center, "NC Opens Shanghai Office," October 12, 2010. *http://www.ncbiotech.org/article/nc-opens-shanghai-office.*

143 Official at North Carolina State Economic Development Representative, telephone interview with Commission staff, August 18, 2014.

144 Official at North Carolina State Economic Development Representative, telephone interview with Commission staff, August 18, 2014.

145 Official at North Carolina State Economic Development Representative, telephone interview with Commission staff, August 18, 2014.

146 WSOCTV.com, "Huntersville Mayor Returns Home from China," May 19, 2013. *http://www.wsoctv.com/news/news/local/huntersville-mayor-returns-home-china/nXwh9/.*

147 Lindsay Liu (Chief Representative, The China Office of Arkansas Economic Development Commission), e-mail to Commission staff, November 2, 2014.

148 Lindsay Liu (Chief Representative, The China Office of Arkansas Economic Development Commission), e-mail to Commission staff, November 2, 2014.

149 Lindsay Liu (Chief Representative, The China Office of Arkansas Economic Development Commission), e-mail to Commission staff, November 2, 2014.

150 Lindsay Liu (Chief Representative, The China Office of Arkansas Economic Development Commission), e-mail to Commission staff, November 2, 2014.

151 Jeffrey King (International Business Manager, Asia-Pacific, Advance Colorado), telephone interview with Commission staff, August 15, 2014.

152 Jeffrey King (International Business Manager, Asia-Pacific, Advance Colorado), telephone interview with Commission staff, August 15, 2014.

153 Jeffrey King (International Business Manager, Asia-Pacific, Advance Colorado), telephone interview with Commission staff, August 15, 2014.

154 Official at Choose New Jersey, interview with Commission staff, August 19, 2014.

155 Official at Choose New Jersey, interview with Commission staff, August 19, 2014.

156 Official at Choose New Jersey, interview with Commission staff, August 19, 2014.

157 Michigan Economic Development Corporation, "Partners." *http://www.michiganbusiness.org/about-medc/partners/.*

158 Official at Michigan Economic Development Corporation, interview with Commission staff, August 27, 2014.

159 Official at Michigan Economic Development Corporation, interview with Commission staff, August 27, 2014.

160 Abigail L. Browning (International Policy, Planning and Partnership International Affairs and Business Development, California Governor's Office of Business and Economic Development), interview with Commission staff, February 3, 2015; State of California, *California Opens Trade and Investment Office in China*, April 11, 2013. *http://gov.ca.gov/news.php?id=17994.*

161 *San Jose Mercury News*, "Governor Jerry Brown Goes to China in Seeking Investment in California," April 7, 2013. *http://www.mercurynews.com/ci_22975110/governor-jerry-brown-goes-china-seeking-investment-california.*

162 David Bolognesi (International Investor Relations, State of California), telephone interview with Commission staff, August 14, 2014.

163 State of California, *Governor Brown and Ministry of Commerce Partner to Boost Bilateral Trade and Investment*, April 9, 2013.

164 Abigail L. Browning (International Policy, Planning and Partnership International Affairs and Business Development, California Governor's Office of Business and Economic Development), interview with Commission staff, February 3, 2015.

165 Abigail L. Browning (International Policy, Planning and Partnership International Affairs and Business Development, California Governor's Office of Business and Economic Development), interview with Commission staff, February 3, 2015.

166 Abigail L. Browning (International Policy, Planning and Partnership International Affairs and Business Development, California Governor's Office of Business and Economic Development), interview with Commission staff, February 3, 2015.

167 John Henry Jackson (Manager for Global Projects, Asia Investment, Mississippi Development Authority), e-mail to Commission staff, October 31, 2014; David Briel (Executive Director, Center for Direct Investment, State of Pennsylvania), e-mail to Commission staff, November 5, 2014.

168 Dennis Pruitt (Vice President of International Business Recruitment, Missouri Partnership), interview with Commission staff, August 18, 2014 and February 3, 2015.

169 Dennis Pruitt (Vice President of International Business Recruitment, Missouri Partnership), interview with Commission staff, August 18, 2014 and February 3, 2015.

[170] Joseph A. Rude (International Trade Office, Iowa Economic Development Authority), e-mail to Commission staff, November 5, 2014.

[171] Matthew Patane, "Muscatine Hotel Deepens Ties with China," *The Des Moines Register*, June 14, 2014.

[172] Export.gov, "SelectUSA - About." *http://export.gov/China/selectusa/index.asp.*

[173] *Shanghai Daily*, "Can-Do City of Dallas Woos Chinese Investors in Tech and Energy-Support," June 29, 2012, via Factiva.

[174] Bradley Gillenwater (Regional Manager for Asia, Maryland Department of Business and Economic Development), interview with Commission staff, February 3, 2015; Abigail L. Browning (International Policy, Planning and Partnership International Affairs and Business Development, California Governor's Office of Business and Economic Development), interview with Commission staff, February 3, 2015.

[175] Bradley Gillenwater (Regional Manager for Asia, Maryland Department of Business and Economic Development), interview with Commission staff, February 3, 2015; Abigail L. Browning (International Policy, Planning and Partnership International Affairs and Business Development, California Governor's Office of Business and Economic Development), interview with Commission staff, February 3, 2015.

[176] Michael Barris, "Southern Hospitality Used to Attract Chinese Investments," *China Daily* (U.S. edition), March 28, 2014, via Factiva.

[177] Lindsay Liu (Chief Representative, The China Office of Arkansas Economic Development Commission), e-mail to Commission staff, November 2, 2014.

[178] Lindsay Liu (Chief Representative, The China Office of Arkansas Economic Development Commission), e-mail to Commission staff, November 2, 2014.

[179] *Shanghai Daily*, "Can-Do City of Dallas Woos Chinese Investors in Tech and Energy-Support," June 29, 2012, via Factiva.

[180] Bradley Gillenwater (Regional Manager for Asia, Maryland Department of Business and Economic Development), interview with Commission staff, August 27, 2014.

[181] Bradley Gillenwater (Regional Manager for Asia, Maryland Department of Business and Economic Development), interview with Commission staff, August 27, 2014.

[182] David Bolognesi (International Investor Relations, State of California), telephone interview with Commission staff, August 14, 2014.

[183] Dennis Pruitt (Vice President of International Business Recruitment, Missouri Partnership), interview with Commission staff, February 3, 2015.

[184] David Bolognesi (International Investor Relations, State of California), telephone interview with Commission staff, August 14, 2014.

[185] State of California, *California Opens Trade and Investment Office in China*, April 11, 2013. *http://gov.ca.gov/news.php?id=17994.*

[186] Bradley Gillenwater (Regional Manager for Asia, Maryland Department of Business and Economic Development), interview with Commission staff, August 18, 2014.

[187] Kai Duh (Director, University of Maryland-China Joint Research Park), interview with Commission staff, August 18, 2014.

[188] Kai Duh (Director, University of Maryland-China Joint Research Park), interview with Commission staff, August 18, 2014.

[189] Kai Duh (Director, University of Maryland-China Joint Research Park), interview with Commission staff, August 18, 2014.

[190] Kai Duh (Director, University of Maryland-China Joint Research Park), interview with Commission staff, August 18, 2014.

[191] Kai Duh (Director, University of Maryland-China Joint Research Park), interview with Commission staff, August 18, 2014.

[192] Kai Duh (Director, University of Maryland-China Joint Research Park), interview with Commission staff, August 18, 2014.